Connected

CONNECTED

A Guide *for* Leading
in a More Human Way

JAMI VARELA

LIONCREST
PUBLISHING

CONNECTED
A Guide for Leading in a More Human Way

FIRST EDITION

ISBN   978-1-5445-4620-9   *Hardcover*
        978-1-5445-4622-3   *Paperback*
        978-1-5445-4621-6   *Ebook*
        978-1-5445-4773-2   *Audiobook*

I dedicate this book to my precious daughter, Ava. She is my raison d'etre. My reason for being and my "why." She is the strongest and closest connection I have in my world. She drives me every day to get up and show up at my best. When my epilepsy gets me down and out, or if I'm just having a stressful day at work, I remind myself that she is my sunshine and I owe it to her to pull myself together, get my priorities in order, and be grateful for each memory I have created with her and will continue to create.

Thank you, dear daughter, for showing me the meaning of life. The value of giving myself in service to others and the greater good. You make me a better person, and you make me want to continue to grow.

CONTENTS

THE STRUGGLE

You're a superstar sales rep, breaking records and gaining an unparalleled reputation for closing deals. Other reps look up to you, and your boss is consistently impressed with your performance. It's inevitable that eventually the company would ask you to transition into leadership, so when the day comes that you're offered a promotion, you're already expecting it. You couldn't be more qualified—or so you think—so you accept the promotion and become a sales manager.

And then everything changes. For the first time in a very long time, you suck at your job. As a sales rep, you were a goal-chasing, deal-closing ace, focused entirely on your own achievements and completely invested in your own success. As a manager, you're no longer a star, you're "support," and almost none of the skills you developed over the years seem to apply.

Rather than feeling like the next logical step forward in your career, the promotion feels like a sudden wild turn into left field. You used to come to work every day feeling confident, knowing what you were doing, but you now find yourself floundering. You were a great sales rep, but you're kind of a crappy sales manager. Your team doesn't seem to like you, and quite frankly, you're becoming less fond of them.

"Why did I ever accept that stupid promotion?" you wonder. "I'm no good at dealing with these sales reps and their endless 'issues.' I wish I was back in my old job. At least then I knew what I was doing."

It's a painful wake-up call, and it's all too common, especially in the world of sales. You're a star performer so you get promoted to management. But the role of leadership is very different from what you did before, so you find yourself failing at it. After years of success, you can no longer figure out how to do your job well. All the shiny sales awards hanging on the wall in your office seem like a cruel joke now.

The company assumed that you would do a good job as a leader because you did a good job in your previous role. However, just because you were a good sales rep doesn't mean you know how to coach, mentor, and manage a team. And when it doesn't come naturally to you, you get increasingly frustrated and begin to second-guess your abilities.

You think, "What in the world happened to me? Why am I struggling so much? I was a winner, and now I kind of feel like a loser."

That mounting frustration inevitably leaks out into your performance. You take it out on your direct reports, which spreads the frustration to the rest of the team. Team performance takes a hit, which begins to impact the bottom line. And that's a *big* problem.

Your transition into management is also difficult for your former peers, all those reps who used to work side-by-side with you. When one of their own suddenly rises from the ranks and begins telling them what to do, it can cause a lot of tension. Your job title might have changed, but they still remember when you were cold-calling and schmoozing prospects in the cubicle zoo right beside them.

So whose fault is it that you're not doing well?

The fact is, companies rarely do a good job of communicating what the transition to leadership is going to look like. The poor, struggling leader receives little training and minimal help. They don't know where to turn, so they keep floundering and flailing about until they come to some tragic end. All of these stories tend to end the same way. Either the leader jumps ship and tries again somewhere else or they decimate their team and get fired.

Jumping ship might seem like a better option for the company. If someone can't cut it as a leader, then it's better for them to move on anyway, right? The company can find someone more qualified to fill the position, and all will eventually be well.

Well, except for the fact that high turnover is incredibly expensive. First, there's the lost productivity as the company tries to fill the position. Then there's the expense of finding and interviewing candidates and bringing a new person into the role. There's also the cost of recruiting and training a new team member and bringing them up to speed, a process that might take up to a year.

Besides the money cost and lost time, there's the damage to morale that happens every time a new leader fails. A revolving door of leadership creates a sense of instability, and an unstable workplace is a miserable workplace. Soon enough, sales reps will start dropping like flies, too. The best reps usually leave first because other companies want them. When good reps leave, it inspires other reps to leave, and over time, it becomes harder and harder to recruit new talent. Candidates look at the company and think, "People are leaving that place in droves. Even their best sales reps ran like they were fleeing a murder scene. There must be something really wrong going on over there."

This creates an ugly cycle that can easily become a death spiral for the entire organization. I've seen this exact scenario play out in a number of companies. Maybe you have, too. Maybe you're caught in the death spiral right now and fighting fiercely to get out of it.

Let's face it, it's easier than ever for people to jump ship. In the age of LinkedIn, recruiters are constantly asking people to switch dance partners, and if they're frustrated, people are going to find it really easy to accept the invitation.

"Why not come and work for us? We're better than the place you're at right now."

"I don't know if you're better, but you can't be worse. I'll give it a try."

In reality, the grass is rarely greener in some other company, and it may turn out to be a bad move. But frustrated sales reps and sales managers are willing to take the gamble, especially if there's no light at the end of the tunnel.

SEEING YOUR STORY IN THE STRUGGLE

Maybe you're seeing your own story somewhere in the midst of all of this. You made the transition from sales rep to sales manager (or, if you're not in sales, from employee to leader), and you're struggling hard. Your amazing skills and experience from before haven't translated into leadership. Your team members don't like you, and you're frequently irritated with them.

You might even spend your evenings scrolling through the job listings on LinkedIn and dreaming of starting over somewhere else. Maybe you look at random houses and apartments on Zillow and think, "Yeah, I'd relocate for the right job. Ooh, this one has a sunroom! I just have to get out of this misery somehow."

Well, I've got some good news. I've been down this frustrating road. I know what it's like to go from a superstar sales rep to an ineffective, struggling sales manager. And I've also learned along the way how to turn things around.

I know you're probably afraid to ask for help. I felt the same way at one time. When you're a leader you want to position yourself as the one with all the answers, someone who has everything under control, but even leaders need advice and encouragement. Too many are suffering in silence, blundering their way toward some dumb decisions that are going to get them fired or do irreparable damage to their professional reputation.

I want to help you avoid all of that. In this book, I'm going to help you turn the ship in a much better direction before it runs aground. The ship I'm talking about is your career, and the passengers on board are all the people you're responsible for. If you go down, they might go down, too. Let's avoid that, shall we?

In the following chapters, I'll show you how to lead with confidence and compassion, overcoming the fear of giving and receiving feedback while identifying your own blind spots and biases. We'll discuss how you can use your own instincts but also ask for help.

You'll learn how to get in touch with your company's mission, when to use the "carrot and stick" approach with your people, and *most* importantly, how to truly care about the people entrusted to your leadership. In my experience, *effective* leaders care deeply about the people they're leading.

In the end, you'll have a much clearer idea of what great leadership looks like, and you'll see the concrete steps you need to take to get there. No more floundering. No more being hated and hating your team. And you'll no longer be stumbling your way toward some catastrophic end.

Chapter One

THE PATH TO COMPASSIONATE LEADERSHIP

"No one cares how much you know, until they know how much you care."

—THEODORE ROOSEVELT

Speaking of stumbling along, that's exactly how I wound up as a sales leader. I never planned on going into sales, much less working my way into a leadership position. Looking back, it makes sense. Even in my early career, I found joy in helping others, and that often led to being given greater responsibility—even if it was just a move from waitress to head waitress. When I got my first sales job, I lasted about a year and a half before I was promoted into a management role.

I struggled, just like so many new sales managers, and felt all the frustrations that are probably already familiar to you. Then a former employee invited me to start working for a Fortune

500 company called Paychex. He said, "You'll love working here so much better. You can make a ton of money as a sales rep."

I was tempted, so I jumped ship and became a sales rep again at this much bigger company. Paychex has a stellar reputation, so my expectations were high. And in many ways, it *was* a much better experience. I really connected with the product I was selling, and as with all of my jobs, I was fully committed to giving my best. When a management position opened up, I put myself forward and got the promotion.

Sadly, this time the transition into leadership was a lot worse. It wasn't the company's fault. I realized quickly that I was completely out of my league. I had the skills to be a good sales rep, but those skills didn't apply to leading a big team in a large company. I'd gone from playing a game of checkers to playing high-level chess, and I knew any decision I made now as a leader could have far-reaching unintended consequences if I wasn't careful.

To make matters worse, my boss was new in his role as well, and managing managers is a whole other can of worms. His transition from managing sales reps to managing managers brought plenty of struggles, and it made our relationship contentious. As the days wore on, I became progressively more miserable. Eventually, I realized I had to say something. Too much was at stake, and at the time, I was a mom to a toddler. I couldn't afford to quit a good-paying job at a great company, so I just had to make it work somehow.

Even though it was scary, I decided to approach my boss and request a meeting with him. On a day when I knew he was in his office, I went to him and said, "Hey, can we sit down and talk for a few minutes? I'm really struggling." It took every ounce of willpower to say it. Who wants to admit to their boss that they're not doing well? But I was desperate enough to take the plunge.

Fortunately, my boss agreed to meet. We sat down together and, over the course of a couple of hours, we discussed everything. I tried to be as respectful as possible, but I was also brutally honest with him.

"Things can't keep going this way," I said. "I feel like you and I are both struggling as leaders, and we're not on the same page. Because we're both frustrated, we often interact as if we were adversaries, but the truth is, I need you! This job is hard, and I have to be able to come to you for advice. I want you to give me *counsel*, not just criticism."

That conversation led my boss to talk to his boss, and eventually they decided that what I really needed, in addition to a healthier dynamic with them, was a mentor. Someone from outside our immediate sphere who could provide unbiased guidance, someone we all trusted and respected.

We came up with a short list of candidates. I spoke to each of them, and then chose the one who seemed like they connected with me the best. I know it sounds a little like *The Bachelor*, and I was deciding which guy was going to get the red rose. However, I was simply trying to find a wise colleague who could provide objective advice when I was struggling as a leader.

The individual who eventually became my mentor is still my friend to this day. He served in the same exact role as me earlier in his career, so he was able to speak to my situation. He understood the challenges I faced in my transition to sales manager, and he taught me a lot. However, he also provided some harsh feedback at times, which I received with an open mind.

One thing he told me was, "You're not being firm enough as a leader. You don't respond strongly when your team members are outside the bounds. You need to be more courageous."

In truth, I was scared of some of my team members, especially the ones with strong personalities. You know how sales reps can be. The really good ones tend to be a bit, shall we say, *intense*, because they are driven, relentless go-getters (also, cocky and really good at winning arguments). So I sometimes shied away from speaking to them about issues. However, in order to be successful, my mentor told me, I had to drop the fear and approach my team openly, honestly, and firmly, but with respect and compassion, seeking what was best for everybody.

When I started doing this, lo and behold, I began to see a change. I started having success as a leader. Compassion, openness, honesty, courage, and respect made a huge difference, and my team's attitude toward me warmed.

And then I was blindsided by a health crisis. I began to experience a strange brain fog and periodic panic attacks. When I finally got checked out, I learned to my horror that I had a brain tumor. I took many months off work on medical leave, went through brain surgery, and then spent a long time recovering. It was a really, really bad year, to put it mildly.

While I was on medical leave, my team members constantly reached out to me and told me, "We want you back. Do whatever you have to do to get better so you can return and lead us again." How many sales teams say that kind of thing to their boss? I think most sales teams would breathe a sigh of relief and say, "Oh, goody, the jerk has left the building."

When I finally returned to my job, I discovered that my sales team was now the third worst team out of dozens of sales teams in the company. Everything had fallen apart in my long absence, and somehow I had to make an impact fast. I applied everything I'd learned from my mentor—the very same tips and techniques I share in this book—and it turned things around almost immediately.

By the next fiscal year, my team had become the number one team in the country. From third worst to national best! I attribute this to leading with authenticity, creating a real connection with my team built on respect and honesty, and leading with courage and compassion. Instead of coming back, seeing the challenge, and telling myself, "Somehow I have to whip this team back into shape," I was able to approach them openly and say, "Hey, we're in this together. You guys stuck with me, and we're going to climb this mountain. We can do it."

FROM MANAGER TO LEADER

So what changed in my leadership approach from those early years of struggle? More than anything, I stopped being simply a "manager" and became a human as well. I built a relationship with my team where they weren't afraid to approach me when they had trouble. I wasn't just pushing people to hit numbers. I was trying to help them achieve their best and feel good about it.

I'm going to dive into this approach a lot deeper in the upcoming chapters, but I'm telling you right now, it creates a much deeper level of loyalty—a loyalty that goes both ways. This, in turn, creates a greater sense of cohesion, stronger commitment from everyone, better outcomes, and happier people across the board.

Yes, you still have to hit those monthly quotas. No system is perfect. But this approach will transform the way you lead and the way people follow you. I've seen it firsthand, and I'll share some of my own stories along the way.

Now, to be clear, this book isn't intended to be an autobiography. I'm not writing a memoir here. I don't plan on selling the movie rights. All I'm trying to do is help all of those new leaders, like you, avoid some of the mistakes that made my early years so painful. Consider it a guidebook for dealing with the pitfalls of leadership.

But it's not just a book about avoiding mistakes. I also want to contribute to your long-term success as a leader. If you're in leadership, part of the reason you're there is to help people. You'll get to the financial goals—everyone will—but if you can be of more service to your team, you're going to get to your goals with a committed and compassionate team. And isn't that what we all want?

Chapter Two

UNLICENSED THERAPIST

"Leadership is not a formula or a program, it is a human activity that comes from the heart and considers the hearts of others."

—LANCE SECRETAN

There's a lot of confusion in the business world about the difference between being a manager and being a leader. The two are not the same, and the difference between them has nothing to do with the job title.

Managers manage things. They focus on getting tasks done. Envision little automaton people standing in front of a vast machine, pulling levers to make widgets. A manager is the one who's strolling about to make sure everyone keeps pulling their respective levers in a timely manner so shiny, new widgets keep tumbling out of the end of the machine.

That's managing, and it's what most "bosses" spend their days doing. They're not worried about the emotional well-being of individual workers because, quite frankly, widget-makers and lever-pullers are easily replaced (no offense to any actual widget makers or lever-pullers out there). You can always find someone else to take their place at the machine and keep production going.

An unusually friendly manager might have some compassion for a worker who is having a bad day, but even then, they probably don't see a direct connection between the emotional well-being of that employee and their productivity. And it's really not their job to worry about it anyway. They just need to make sure people keep pulling those levers and efficiently churning out widgets to meet quotas.

In the world of sales, this approach creates a real problem, because the sales manager establishes a relationship dynamic that sales reps emulate. As a manager, you're dealing with people all day long, and if you treat them like lever-pulling automatons, they're going to treat prospective clients the same way (with hard-sell tactics, manipulation, lack of empathy, and so forth).

You'll never get the best out of people this way, not from employees, not from clients, not from the barista at the corner coffee shop on your lunch break. *Nobody likes to be treated like an automaton.*

What sales reps really need is *authentic human leadership*. A leader cares about their people—not just hitting quotas and churning out widgets, but the actual mental and emotional well-being of the people entrusted to them. And if you genuinely care about your reps, then they're going to model that genuine care to prospective clients.

THE WAY IT USED TO BE

Look, managing the lever-pullers worked pretty well thirty or forty years ago. At least, people expected it back then. They came to work, behaved like good little robots, and if they fell behind, they expected the boss to yell at them. That was just how it went. Your boss didn't have to like you, and you didn't expect them to care about your feelings.

I don't think anyone ever *enjoyed* this kind of leadership, but they certainly put up with it as a normal part of having a job. But I'll tell you right now, people do not respond well to this kind of standoffish, cold management style anymore. You're not going to get good little drones out of the current generation; you're going to get high turnover and people who hate you. Sales reps won't like it, and prospects will view your company as cold and unfriendly.

If you truly want to *lead*, you're going to have to care about the emotional well-being of your people. It's as simple as that. Look, in my opinion, this has been a great change for the workplace. Society as a whole is better off when companies consider the well-being of employees. You're going to create a healthier work environment and you're going to get more productivity out of people when they no longer feel dehumanized at work.

It's a win–win. Actually, it's a win–win–win, right? You win because the people you're leading will be more engaged and productive at work. Employees win because they feel like their leaders want them to thrive and do well. And your clients and prospective clients win because your genuine compassion rubs off on employees.

But here's the thing. To truly model compassion as a leader, you're sometimes going to have to operate like an unlicensed therapist. Your team members don't leave their personal pain at the door. If a sales rep is grieving at home, they're going to grieve at work. If a sales rep is going through a nasty, stressful divorce at home, they're going to be stressed out about it at work.

The old-fashioned manager expected employees to suck it up and dump all of those personal problems at the door of the office park. Let's be honest. Nobody was ever really able to do this, not completely, but they usually tried. The grieving sales rep would grit his teeth and man those phones and just try not to let the crushing sadness seep into his voice. He didn't always succeed.

People these days can see how screwed up that approach is, and they just won't go along with it. The workforce today is not going to pretend like nothing's wrong if their personal life is hell. The harder you try to keep personal emotions out of the workplace, the worse your team will perform and the worse your relationship with them will be.

It's kind of a sick, twisted thing to do anyway. Trying to get frustrated, sad, stressed, miserable people to pretend like nothing is wrong, to plaster a smile on their faces and fake it, is really weird when you think about it. That approach needed to change, and we should all be glad that it *has* changed.

So, as a leader, you have to project that work is a safe space for hurting team members. You care. Their team cares. And if you can help, you're going to help. That might mean just sitting down with a hurting team member for a bit and letting them vent, offering some comfort and maybe even a bit of advice. Maybe you think, "I didn't sign up for this." Oh, yes, you did! You signed up to be a leader, and this is what leaders do. They lead with compassion.

Now, of course, there are limitations. You can't solve everyone's problems. You're probably not going to sit down with an employee whose marriage is falling apart and tell them how to save their marriage. You're not going to provide unqualified financial advice to a sales rep who is dealing with the painful consequences of bad money choices.

In fact, for serious personal problems, it's a better idea to offer resources to employees like an employee assistance program (EAP) or FinFit. Listen to them, be compassionate, then point them in the right direction (toward qualified professional help).

If you don't create a safe space for employees to talk to you, they're going to talk to *someone*, and besides wasting time, they might go to the wrong person. Bad employees are a bit like lobsters in a lobster pot. When one lobster tries to get out of the boiling water, the bad lobsters will pull them right back in. Instead of comforting or encouraging the hurting employee, a bad lobster might just poison their thinking and make it worse.

It's far better to create an environment where people know their leader actually cares about them, and heck, you might even help them resolve some of their problems. At the very least, you can reassure them that there's light at the end of the tunnel because they're not going to get fired for having trouble in their personal lives. It's hard enough when your life is falling apart, but it's a whole lot worse when you know your sadness puts your job in jeopardy. Suddenly, the poor soul who is grieving a loss also has to worry that his suboptimal attitude at work will also result in a loss of income. That's cruel.

Nobody has time for a workplace like that. What kind of a crappy human being do you have to be to fire someone who is in terrible pain just because they can't pull the damned lever on your widget machine as fast as they used to? Be a human and show a bit of compassion. Be an unlicensed therapist and listen to them. Try to point them to resources that will help, if you can.

If you're not a good listener, then that's a skill you should work on. Don't interrupt or talk over people, just listen. You know how the sales reps who struggle to close deals are generally the ones who don't listen to clients, who talk over them constantly? The same goes for leaders.

Maybe you're not sure if you're a good listener or not. Go ask your employees, managers, and colleagues for feedback. This can be as simple as asking, "On a scale of one to ten, how would you grade me as a listener?" If the number is low, you've got some work to do. Chances are, you probably talk too much. Remember, a good therapist listens carefully and patiently *before* offering advice. Train yourself to do the same.

I'm telling you right now, if you will take a more human approach, your team is going to respond a heck of a lot better, and it's going to be reflected in their performance over the long term.

FIX YOURSELF FIRST

Of course, if you're going to help other people, you're going to have to do some work on yourself as well. An emotionally unhealthy person isn't going to be much help to another emotionally damaged person. If you'll learn to deal with your own emotions, you will be more able to care for others.

Don't be afraid to ask for help! As we'll discuss a little later, it's important for you to find mentors or trusted colleagues that you can turn to when you're struggling in your own life. Just watch out for the bad lobsters because confiding in the wrong person can drag you down ever farther in the darkness.

It's important to deal with your own problems because otherwise you might start dumping your baggage on your sales reps when they come to you for help. You're the leader. You're there to listen to them, not to pile your problem onto their backs.

Recently, I went on a long road trip with my daughter and a friend of hers, and since we had plenty of time, we talked a lot about our lives and plans for the future. At one point, in regard to making important decisions, my daughter said, "Yeah, I just totally trust my gut and follow my instincts."

And I snapped back, "But what if your instincts suck?"

I wasn't trying to insult her. It's a valid concern. I mean, when the creepy guy rolls through town in the windowless van, some people's instinct tells them to take the candy and get in the van, right? We can't always trust what our gut tells us to do. The same certainly holds true for leaders, even good leaders, which is another reason you need your own support system. You need someone who can keep you in check.

Remember, while you sometimes have to be an unlicensed therapist for your employees, they cannot—and should not—be therapists for you. *You can't confide in the people you lead the way they confide in you.* That creates an unhealthy leadership dynamic and might undermine your authority. It also might get your employees gossiping about you:

"Man, did you hear what's going on with the boss? It's crazy! Her marriage is on the rocks, and she totaled her car last week. What a mess. I can't believe she's in charge."

Your own boss can't play this role for you either. That could be political or career suicide. Find yourself a strong support network of peers, colleagues, and mentors that you can speak freely to, people who aren't going to use your words to bury you later. Maybe they even possess some skills or expertise in areas where you struggle. Be intentional about who you select.

Know your lane! Go to colleagues, not your employees and not your boss, for your own emotional support.

This is common sense, though. Think about it. When you go to a therapist, you don't expect her to confide in you. She's there to listen to you and give support and advice. It's not a two-way street. Can you imagine if your therapist said, "Well, now that you've told me all about your problems with your mother, let me tell you all about *my* problems with *my* mother. Then we can trade advice."

That wouldn't work. Actually, you might just run out of the therapist's office. As a leader, sometimes you're going to provide emotional support and a bit of unlicensed therapy to the people you lead, but it shouldn't go both ways. Get your support from peers and mentors.

A BIT OF BALANCE

Now, you can take the therapy thing too far, so find a healthy balance. You're not *actually* a therapist, so you need to put some reasonable boundaries in place. That's why I called you an *unlicensed* therapist.

You're not the right person to solve your team members' deep needs. As I said, if someone needs real help, point them to an employee assistance program. Pull out a business card for the EAP with the phone number on it and hand it to them. Or point them to whatever other agency, financial advisor, marriage counselor, or mental health professional can help them deal with their very real problem, whatever it may be.

If Bob comes to you and says, "Boss, my finances are in tatters. I bought one too many collectible figurines, and now I'm deep in debt. What should I do? Should I file for bankruptcy?" it's not your job to provide him with an answer. Express empathy and point Bob in the direction of real, qualified financial help.

By the way, *empathy* is different than *sympathy*. Empathy means putting yourself in someone else's shoes, trying to understand their feelings and see things from their perspective, not just feeling compassion for them. You should always strive for empathy with your team members, but that doesn't mean providing answers you're unqualified to provide.

An employee might come to you and say, "I'm thinking

about getting a divorce. My husband is a loser. What should I do?" Don't tell them what to do about their marriage. They need to speak to a marriage counselor or therapist. Quite frankly, you're probably stressed enough about work, so you're liable to say something stupid. Even worse, you might start talking about your own problems. "Oh, yeah, I'm getting a divorce, too! Let's share horror stories about our spouses."

It's one thing to say, "I know how you feel. I've been through it." Put yourself in their shoes, express empathy. That's fine. It becomes a problem when you start positioning yourself as an expert, or when you say things that make the situation worse. Remember, you're not trying to create a boss/buddy relationship. You're simply showing sincere concern for the mental and emotional well-being of your team members.

Don't pretend like you have all the answers, because if you give an employee bad advice and make things worse, they'll hold it against you forever. Listen to them, express empathy, and point them to a company program, if it's appropriate.

So, yes, there are times when an effective leader has to act like an unlicensed therapist, but know your boundaries, stay in your lane, and point people to real help. You want employees to feel like it's safe for them to bring things to you. You're a safe space when they're stressed out or hurting. You will listen, you will care, and you will point them to real help when they need it.

People bring their whole selves to work, whether they intend to or not, so check in with them. Ask how they're doing and mean it! Don't punish people for not leaving all of their personal pain at the office door. They're human beings. If you wanted to work with automatons or robots, you got in the wrong line of work.

Chapter Three

GOLDEN GLOBE BEST SUPPORTING ACTOR

"As a leader, what type of shadow will you cast?"

—ANONYMOUS

Hey, even if you're the best leader in the world, there are going to be some days when you don't feel like your best self. It's hard to be the empathetic unlicensed therapist when you're having a bad day, but your people still need you to be there for them. They're counting on you to create a workplace where they can thrive.

There's no getting around it. Some days, you're just going to have to compartmentalize a little bit. As we said before, you can't expect your employees, the people under your leadership, to become your therapists. You can't go to them for emotional support. That creates an unhealthy workplace dynamic that will undermine your authority.

You're there to support *them*, even if you don't feel like it in the moment. I'm sorry, but there are going to be days when you have to be the Golden Globe–winning best supporting actor for the sake of your team's well-being. I'm not saying you need to be fake. I'm saying you need to show up as your best self, even if you're not feeling like your best self.

This is a calling of leadership, and it's not always easy. It's especially true when you're a sales manager. As a sales manager, you are constantly modeling the attitude and approach that you want your sales reps to adopt with prospects. How you treat reps, how you act around them, will inform the way they act on sales calls. You set the tone.

If you're going through a bad time in your personal life, you might have to put a few things in a compartment for a while. It's okay to be a little bit vulnerable, to tell someone at work that you're having a bad day, but you can't open yourself wide and let all of your emotional baggage spill out.

There may be some times when you get out of a meeting with someone and think, "God, I feel like I was full of it. I was just acting the whole time." Well, you're not full of it. You're simply putting your best self out there, even if you don't feel like it today. That's okay. And if you're a natural leader, you probably draw energy from helping your employees, so lean into that. Award-winning actors feel energized when they play a role really well. There's nothing wrong with that, and some days you're going to have to do it, too. In fact, the people you lead need it from you!

MY BEST PERFORMANCE

At this point, I'm sure we all have pandemic horror stories to share. Everyone was scared, and businesses were scrambling to figure out how to handle it. At Paychex, we were worried about the future. How were we supposed to navigate the pandemic without completely shutting down?

We were afraid, our clients were afraid. People were dying, and the future seemed bleak. As a leader, somehow I had to figure out how to stay healthy myself and make sure my people stayed healthy without lecturing them too much or getting too political. To make matters worse, we were selling HR outsourcing, so our sales reps were going into an environment where businesses were struggling to navigate all of these awful things.

The economy as a whole was limping along, but here's the thing: we knew that our product could genuinely help all of these struggling companies. If we could sell our product, we might make a positive impact on the economy in a time of trouble. Suddenly, what we did for a living became part of a much bigger mission.

So I worked all of this into my message to my team. I set all of my own worries aside and got them to view their jobs as part of this greater mission to save the economy. I compartmentalized my fear and communicated a message of hope and purpose; I gave an award-winning performance, and it was hugely successful.

My sales reps were able to get past their fears, and they went above and beyond the call of duty. I told them, "You're going to be speaking to business owners who are terrified on at least five different levels, and you need to tell them, 'We've got you. Paychex has got you!'"

My Golden Globe performance rubbed off on them, and they were able to take that same inspirational message to prospective clients. But to get that performance, I had to dig deep and create a message that sold the idea that we were doing more than just making sales. We were on a mission during a time of need! That message and my impassioned performance made a huge positive impact during the pandemic.

YOUR SET THE MOOD

There's a quote on emotional intelligence that seems appropriate here: "What shadow are you going to cast?" As a leader, you cast a shadow that covers your entire team and affects their performance. You set the tone. You create the environment. So what sort of energy are you bringing?

You can't just dump all of your personal emotional garbage into the middle of the room and say, "Good luck, team. Sell a lot of widgets today!" If you need to offload some baggage, as I said before, get your own support network of colleagues, peers, and mentors.

Now, to be fair, some leaders don't realize that they're bringing negative energy into the workplace. To avoid that, you need to check in with yourself and your own support network regularly to make sure you're not showing up negatively to your team. I'm sorry to say, you might need to work on your acting performance a little more. Currently, you might not be up for any awards, and your team can see right through you to your heart of despair.

To be clear, I'm not saying you should be fake. People can see right through that, too. All I'm saying is you can't go to your employees for emotional support. They can't be there to help you get through your stress, frustration, sadness, or whatever it might be.

If you come to work in a bad mood, you have to dig deep and be the leader that your team needs. You can even tell them you're having a bad day, as long as you then act like the leader they need you to be.

THE WRONG MESSAGE AT THE WRONG TIME

When the pandemic hit hard in March of 2020, we were located in one of the first parts of the country to experience lockdowns. Normally, we sent out emails every day that showed the sales rankings in categories like "number of appointments." If it was green, it meant that rep was hitting or exceeding their numbers. Yellow meant they were on the line. And red meant they missed the mark.

When lockdowns began, my boss continued sending out these emails. However, I started getting feedback from distraught employees because everyone was slipping into the yellow and red. Social distancing and lockdowns meant a lot of clients were in a holding pattern, and it was practically impossible for reps to hit their sales numbers.

"What are we supposed to do?" my team kept asking me. "It's impossible to hit green with everything that's going on!"

Finally, one evening after work, I called my boss, and we talked for a good ninety minutes.

"Hey, I need to talk to you about something that's bothering me," I said. "I'm afraid we're trying to do business as usual while the world is falling into chaos around us. Why do we continue to send out these ranking emails without any context?"

"Well," he replied, "I just want to keep everyone focused. Yes, it's business as usual, because after all, your car payment doesn't go away, your mortgage or rent payment doesn't go away. We still have to do business. We still have to report to Wall Street every day."

"Yeah, that's true," I conceded, "but this pandemic is so new, we don't know how it's going to play out. We don't know if any of our people are ill, if they have family members who are ill. Everybody is freaking out, and they're just getting green, yellow, red in their inbox every night. I know we have to report to Wall Street, but do our people have to feel the heat? We've got to show our sales reps some compassion. They are working under historically difficult circumstances. The status quo of our ranking emails has to change. Let's give them a chance to catch their breath."

At first, the boss chuckled and said, "Oh, God, you and your sympathy!"

"No, it's not sympathy," I replied. "It's *empathy*! Feel what they're going through right now. We need to empower these people to keep showing up, but our approach has to change. We're pushing them to cold call clients in the midst of lock-downs, when businesses are in full-blown panic mode. Nobody wants to be sold anything right now, and if we keep pressuring our people with these emails, we're only going to push more prospects away."

"But we're running a business," he said. "Nobody benefits if we stop selling."

"True," I said, "but we need to craft a message for our team that really inspires them. Tell them, 'Hey, this is an unprece-dented time, so we're going to take a break from sending you the weekly rankings. Instead, we're going to figure out a way to *help* our clients, not just sell to them. We'll help them see the value of what we offer in the midst of this crisis, and we're going to help keep them from having to close their doors.'"

In the end, I got through to him. He realized that what we communicated at that time, the way we conveyed hope and rose to the occasion, was going to make all the difference. So a message was crafted to that end—it was quite moving, I must say—and it made a huge positive impact. By showing our reps that we were empathetic, hopeful, and optimistic, we were able to keep the company going during the worst of the pandemic.

Even more, that attitude rubbed off on reps, who then

brought it to our clients. Many clients who were in despair, on the verge of shutting down, responded strongly to that message. In the long run, it made a big difference in their success and our success. But it required leaders to grit their teeth, compartmentalize their own fears for a minute, and put on a great and inspirational performance.

That's part of your job and your calling as a leader.

Chapter Four

DON'T BRING FEAR TO THE VILLAGE PEOPLE

"People may hear your words, but they feel your attitude."

—JOHN C. MAXWELL

As a leader, you have the weight of the world on your shoulders. You have to direct, guide, and care about your team, but you also have to answer to the leaders above you. And sometimes, your boss and your boss's boss will dump a whole lot of stress down upon you. When you get pressure from above, it's tempting to pass it along to your team and just start lighting people up.

"Hey, team, you've got to pick up the pace because I've got executives breathing down my neck! They're freaking out up there in the C-suite, so come on!"

Don't do it. Never do this. Never, ever do this.

Your own leaders might scare you from time to time, but if it doesn't feel good for you, it certainly won't feel good for your team. Don't pass your fear down the chain of command to the people below you. It will devastate your team, and again, it undermines your authority.

You have to act like an oil filter, catching the gunk that flows down from above and preventing it from getting to your team.

Whether you're in a publicly traded company or a mom-and-pop business, messaging can come down to you from above that's harsh, but it's your job to handle it. Don't automatically pass it down the line. If it's a harsh message that you *have* to pass down the line, you might need to soften it first.

Now, of course, you can't filter so many things that you're no longer in line with the company leadership or mission statement. Sometimes, you have to deliver the message, whether you want to or not. That's what you're hired to do. So don't hide information that your leaders want your team to know.

However, a good leader knows when something coming from above is too scary, when it's likely to demoralize the team the way it's written. If you can't filter the message, if you can't soften it because you're expected to deliver the message *as is*, then you can at least open with a statement that will brace your team.

It's the equivalent of saying, "Hey, folks, I have to rip the Band-Aid off now. This might hurt to hear, but you need to know where we're at and what we're going to do about it." In other words, preface the harsh message so your people won't be caught entirely off guard. That will make it easier to begin digesting it, because they're not just getting hit over the head without warning.

MESSAGES FROM THE HEART

Difficult messaging starts with the heart. If you have to deliver some bad news or deal with a troubling situation, couch the message in compassion: "We need to discuss this because the results are important for everyone to know. You're not in trouble, and this isn't about someone being bad. There are simply some things we need to do, as individuals and as an organization, and if we do them, everyone will benefit."

I'm not recommending these exact words. Rather, I'm saying you can frame a difficult message in concern for the well-being of your people—sincerely, not faking it—and they will be more receptive to hearing it. More than that, they won't feel demoralized by it.

Also, make sure you understand the message that you're supposed to pass along before you deliver it. Ask some clarifying questions of your leader. Let them know that you're not comfortable delivering the message as is and need a better understanding of what results the message is intended to achieve. Sometimes, simply understanding the desired results will enable you to pass the message down the line without scaring your team.

It will also help you identify the parts of the message that need to be filtered, those sharp edges that won't contribute to the results and might actually be counterproductive. Just don't dilute the message so much that it obscures company objectives. As I mentioned earlier, too much filter puts you out of step with company leaders. The goal here is not to create misalignment but simply to ensure you're not dumping unnecessary amounts of fear and stress down upon your team.

If you're in fear, you will show up in fear. So if your leaders are scaring you or stressing you out, go to your own direct supervisor and gain some clarity. See if you can't work out more effective messaging that's not going to terrify your team. Advocate for your team! Most supervisors want to avoid demoralizing employees, so they'll probably work with you to soften some of the too-sharp edges.

CHECK IN WITH YOUR PEOPLE

When people are afraid at work, they tend to withdraw. They're probably not going to come to you and say, "Hey, boss, I'm getting scared by some of the stuff you're saying," or "Hey, boss, your fear is kind of rubbing off on me." Instead, they'll just go silent. Oh, they'll commiserate with peers and fellow employees, but they won't say anything to *you*.

You might not even be aware of the negative impact you're having on them, so you're going to have to check in with them from time to time—especially when you're getting heat from up above. And when you deliver a message, make sure *they* understand it, understand the intended results, and haven't been paralyzed by fear because of it.

If it's a really challenging message that calls for extreme change, you need to check in very soon after you've delivered it—and again later on—and do it *individually*. People won't always speak their mind in a group setting, but if you talk to them one-on-one and provide a safe space for them to talk through their fears and concerns, you're far more likely to get to a healthy outcome.

Whatever you do, never, ever put people on blast in a group setting for expressing concerns about a message. That's sure to be disastrous. At the very least, it discourages people from being honest, sharing their concerns, or speaking at all. They'll think, "Boss tore my head off! Next time, I'll keep my worries to myself."

If you deliver the message in a group setting, you can take questions but then add, "I know some of you may not be comfortable asking questions or expressing concerns here. That's fine. We can talk about it one-on-one." Give people permission to speak or not to speak. Most employees hate being called on in a group setting. When you do this, they tend to go into robot mode and give blank assent—"I liked the message; it was fine"—even if they're trembling inside.

Again, a lot of this comes down to the way you deliver the message. Even if you have to deliver bad news, you can do it thoughtfully and empathetically. Your people will love you for it. Yes, they'll love you even if you're bringing them bad news, because people love empathy from their leaders. From their perspective, you're keeping it real and showing genuine concern for them.

DO WHAT YOU CAN

Fear shuts people down. The primitive brain reacts to scary messages and puts people in "fight or flight" mode. So if you get fear from above, you don't necessarily have to pass it along.

Filter what you can. Frame what you can. Clarify the message with your own boss. Express honest concern and compassion. Check in with your people afterward, and give them safe space to ask questions and express their worries or fears.

Remember, every person in the chain of command all the way up to the CEO is a human being, and we all struggle with fear. If you love your organization, if you love what you sell, then you do what you can to help everyone thrive. When a scary message comes down from above, just remind yourself that you're dealing with people. Have compassion in both directions, and you'll be a better leader all around.

.... *Chapter Five* ....

"1980 CALLED. THEY WANT THEIR LEADERSHIP STYLE BACK...AND THEIR POWER SUIT!"

"Leadership is an ever-evolving position."

—MIKE KRZYZEWSKI

I started working at Paychex back in 2006. I vividly recall taking my first trip to the corporate office out in Rochester, because I was required to wear pantyhose. That was a rule in the company at the time. I remember thinking, "Pantyhose? Seriously? In this day and age?" But I went along with it, as uncomfortable as it was.

There were a few other antiquated rules at the time. If an employee had tattoos, they had to completely cover them. If they had a nose ring, they had to take it out and put a Band-

Aid over the hole. I mean, the company culture at that time was stuck in the age of power suits and shoulder pads, let me tell you! We've come a long way.

I had a mentor, now retired, who worked at Paychex for thirty years. When she finally retired, she told me, "Hey, when I started here, I wasn't even allowed to wear pants. That's how far we've come." This isn't a knock against the company, by any means. It's a great place to work, and it has become an absolutely amazing company culture. I only mention it because sometimes companies are a little slow to adjust their leadership style, even as a changing culture makes it less effective.

It's a mild example of a leadership struggle that I see out in the business world: leaders who are still trying to lead the way they have always led, even though younger workers no longer respond well to it.

Sometimes, we're not intentionally trying to use old-fashioned leadership styles, but we're unaware of our own unconscious biases and behaviors that were ingrained in us long ago. I see this play out with my sales reps sometimes. For example, sometimes I'll notice that a rep's clients all look just like them, even though the culture they're selling in has become far more diverse over the last couple of decades. They're not intentionally trying to be narrow-minded, but they've gotten used to reaching out to one type of person, so they just keep doing it. When it happens with one of my sales reps, I like to remind them, "You know, it might be nice to learn something about other cultures. Broaden your reach a bit."

This still happens in hiring practices in some companies (thankfully, not Paychex). Leaders hire essentially one kind of person, because that's the kind of person they've always hired. That's the image they have in their mind of what their workforce is supposed to look like. Sometimes leaders like to hire mirror images of themselves. They might even say things like, "Wow, this candidate reminds me of myself when I was a young and ambitious sales rep."

Hiring only people who look like you may have been an acceptable thing to do a few decades ago. But if you hire only people who look like you, you'll wind up with clients who only look like you. And that just doesn't fly with most of the general public today. People, especially young people, don't respond favorably to a company that doesn't reflect the growing diversity of the world around us. The young talent you're trying to recruit expects your workforce *and* your client list to be diverse.

The power suit is dead, but also, people now come in all shapes and sizes. They always did, of course, but the workplace has finally caught on.

Over the last twenty years, there has been a real evolution in leadership and the work environment that leaders create. Those changes have touched everything from dress codes to management styles. Almost everything has changed, but not everyone got the memo.

If you work in an organization that is already on the fast track to change, consider yourself lucky. If they've already embraced changing dress codes, management styles, and diversity, that's great. If you're *not* in an organization like that, perhaps you can influence change.

If nothing else, you can create your own little area of diversity and empathetic leadership within your sphere of influence. Don't hire your mirror image. Intentionally try to create a team that is diverse in many ways, and encourage reps to reach out to diverse prospects.

You will learn so much from your diverse team members. It will make you a better leader, and it will create a more engaged and committed team, especially with your younger employees.

THINGS CHANGE. DEAL WITH IT.

Unfortunately, there's still a lot of old-fashioned leadership advice floating around out there, so beware. Old-fashioned leadership was about exerting control rather than giving support, and you're not in the business of controlling people. That's old school.

Old-fashioned leadership teaches people *what* to think rather than teaching them *how* to think. It creates systems and processes that are meant to govern behavior and force people into certain actions, rather than guiding and strengthening people to give their best. It lacks empathy, doesn't care about feelings, and focuses almost exclusively on conformity. Friends, that approach to leadership might have worked forty years ago, but it sure as hell doesn't work with the current generation.

Quite frankly, a lot of older leaders are learning the hard way that old-fashioned leadership no longer works, and they're struggling to figure out how to adjust. There's a reason why TED Talks on emotional intelligence are so popular in leadership right now. You have to abandon that old, antiquated idea of what a "boss" looks like. The title alone doesn't give you authority or respect.

Under the old view, a boss was someone who sat in a big chair behind a big desk and barked out orders. Your workforce will resist and resent you with every fiber of their being if you're still trying to lead like this. Modern leaders practice true engagement with their workforce. They guide, support, and encourage; reward results; and address shortcomings with compassion (when possible).

If you're not evolving as a leader, you're running out of time. There's no time to adapt slowly because the young employees of today would rather not work at all than put up with an old-fashioned "boss." As Darwin put it, "It is not the strongest of the species that survives, nor the most intelligent that survives. It is the one that is most adaptable to change." We can say the same exact thing about leaders.

We're all aware of how fast the technological landscape has changed in recent decades. Some of us have seen it. We grew up going to the library and using the card catalog and the Dewey decimal system to find books and check them out so we could learn new things. Now, we pull out our phones and open an app to gain access to all the knowledge in the world. That's a massive change in my lifetime.

But here's the thing: leadership has changed just as much! If you try to lead young people today like an old boss would have, they're going to laugh at you behind your back. They're going to mock you in the break room and on social media. And they're going to resist, resist, resist.

This is your employee pool! There's no avoiding it. Learn to lead them effectively, or you're going to flounder. I know, sometimes it's a struggle. Some of us have struggled to adapt to technological change in our personal lives, so of course we're going to struggle to adapt as leaders. I've had to go to my kids at times and say, "Hey, how do I work this newfangled thing?" First, they mock me a little bit, but then they show me how to make it work.

Some of us also have to relearn how to be leaders, even though we've been leaders for years. I was a year old when Paychex started back in 1971. There aren't a lot of fifty-two-year-old companies still in operation. How have they managed to keep going? Simple: They've adapted to change.

If you adapt, you keep growing and thriving. If you dig in your heels, you stagnate and die. It's that simple. If your current leadership hasn't figured this out, you need to help them see it. As a leader yourself, you need to grow and learn. Become a voracious reader, Googler, and TED Talker. Do everything you can to increase your emotional intelligence.

INCREASE YOUR EMOTIONAL INTELLIGENCE

So what's a good starting place? If you want to start adapting and increasing your emotional intelligence (EQ), survey your employees. Conduct a 360 review, where you gather anonymous feedback from your people and let them rate various categories or aspects of your leadership. Reading the results can be rough, and it might serve as a wakeup call about some stuff that you didn't know you need to change.

Also, don't be afraid of personality tests. They'll help you learn some things about yourself. You might even request to conduct a personality test with your own boss as a way of starting a conversation. Now, that might scare you a bit, but if you're afraid to even start the conversation about your leadership style, something's really wrong. What are you afraid to learn about yourself?

Everyone has to grow and adapt. Leaders in every industry are having to make changes in order to effectively lead their workforce. Heck, even the US military has been accused of being "woke" because they're trying to adapt and lead young adults effectively, and the old hard-ass approach doesn't work anymore. Simon Sinek gave a great talk about how the Navy SEALs are adapting to change by embracing a servant leadership approach that is based on trust rather than rigid, harsh authority.[1] The red-faced, screaming drill instructor doesn't get

---

1 See "What the Navy SEALs Can Teach Businesses About Team-Building," The Optimism Company (July 7, 2023), https://simonsinek.com/stories/what-the-navy-seals-can-teach-businesses-about-team-building.

through to Gen Z and will never inspire them, no matter how much old people romanticize it.

The cigar-chomping boss behind the big desk who has steam coming out of his ears will never, ever create an engaged, high-functioning workforce.

Leadership has changed. Culture has changed. The world has changed. Deal with it.

Sometimes, your highest performer is not the person you want to put in leadership, because the ferocity with which they pursue results won't translate well to leading a team in this day and age. To put it bluntly, nobody wants to work for an asshole. What people are looking for now is someone they can trust. Effective leaders inspire trust in their team.

I'll say it again. Not fear. Trust. You're going to have to adapt to this change, or you will never be an effective leader, no matter what structures or processes you put in place.

Never be afraid to buck the status quo of an older leadership style, but do it respectfully. If you're stuck in a company that's still using an outdated style of leadership and you're not high enough in the organization to implement change, you first need to ask yourself if you're in the right home. Mid-level managers can't come in and start acting like the vice president, so figure out if you need to stay there. Nobody deserves to be stuck in a toxic workplace.

What's a good sign that you're not in the right place? The Sunday Scaries. When four o'clock on Sunday afternoon rolls around, do you start feeling dread? Are you in tears because another work week is right around the corner? Nobody should feel that way about work, but that's what happens when you're powerless in an old, toxic system.

Then again, you might be able to implement *some* changes, even if you're not at the top. Start within your own sphere of influence. See what you can inspire. Adapt, grow, and evolve as a leader. Increase your own emotional intelligence, and see what impact you can make. Focus on building trust instead of fear. You might be amazed at the difference in how your people respond to you.

Chapter Six

THE ART OF HUMANING

"There is no more noble occupation in the world than to assist another human being—to help someone succeed."

—ALAN LOY MCGINNIS

There's a whole big messy world out there. When employees walk through the doors of your building, they bring a wide array of baggage with them. Some of those people—maybe all of them—are dealing with awful things in their personal lives.

This is true everywhere, in every business, in every industry. When people come to work, they bring their messy selves with them. A good leader understands this and empathizes with people. More than that, a truly effective leader knows how to sort through the mess with them so they can take care of business, always leaving enough room for their humanity to remain intact.

It wasn't always this way in the workplace. In some companies, it's *still* not this way. The old-fashioned style of leadership expects everyone to leave all of their personal junk at home. Grieving the loss of a loved one? Going through a painful divorce? Having financial problems at home? Worried about one of your kids? It doesn't matter. There's no room for personal feelings, thoughts, or emotional struggles in the workplace. You take all of that off in the morning like a rumpled t-shirt, put your business attire on, straighten your tie, and come to work calm, cool, and collected. Otherwise, Mr. Big Boss is going to give you an earful.

That's how it used to be, and for some leaders, that's how it still is. At the very least, even if they don't scold employees for bringing their personal baggage to work, they will do their best to ignore and neglect a suffering employee. Oh, they'll respond if it's affecting job performance, of course, in which case escalating consequences will be meted out.

"You will suffer my wrath until you calm down." That's the idea. Or, as they like to put it, "Be professional."

And as we've already said, that kind of leadership is a fast track to high turnover, a toxic work environment, and a lot of resentful employees who have no respect for you.

GIVE THEM A LITTLE SPACE

When I returned to work after my first brain surgery, I was forced to work from home so I could juggle work responsibilities with my self-care and recovery. I got a call from my boss one day, who told me that a certain executive whom I had never met was coming to town to meet with me. He didn't know me, didn't know what all I'd been through, and hadn't been informed that I was working from home.

"Never fear. He doesn't care about your personal stuff," my boss said. "Just know your sales numbers. We'll be meeting in the office, so put on your best Fox News work dress and get yourself here."

Well, that was easier said than done, but I took off the pajamas I'd been wearing every day of my recovery, put on some professional attire, and dragged myself into the office to meet with the executive. The meeting went fine, and I didn't let on how difficult it was for me. We got past my sales numbers pretty quickly, and the executive began asking about my personal life. When I told him how many times I'd been to the emergency room in the previous ten months, his jaw dropped.

"You're kidding me," he said. "How are you doing this? How are you here today?"

"To be honest, the engagement of working helps a lot with my recovery," I said. "I like what I do."

"Yeah, but how are you coming into the office every day?" he said.

I had no choice but to let the cat out of the bag. "I'm working from home."

Thankfully, he didn't seem miffed by this. "Oh, I see. And what's it like working from home? Does it make things easier?"

Instead of answering right away, I asked him a question: "Does your wife work?"

"No, she's a stay-at-home mom," he said.

"Okay," I said, "so imagine I'm doing your job *and* her job at the same time all day long—while also dealing with my health. That's how it's going. But you've seen my numbers. They're decent."

He nodded gravely. "That is such an amazing perspective," he said. "I didn't realize how much you had to deal with in your personal life. That makes your numbers a lot more impressive. Thanks."

A little glimpse into my personal hell provided some important perspective to an executive that cast my work performance in a different light. Here's the thing: a *lot* of people are walking away from whatever's on fire at home in order to get to the office and start getting work done, but that doesn't mean they've forgotten about what's happening at home. That doesn't mean they're not still feeling the stress, pain, sadness, or whatever.

If you want to be an effective leader, give your people some space for their personal baggage. *Forget the art of the deal; learn the art of humaning!* Bring your humanity into the workplace. Give them space to be human, to live with their authentic selves and not try to suppress everything they're feeling.

We treat employees as if they exist in a vacuum, as if nothing from outside their work cubicle should touch them, impact their performance, or ever be an issue at work. That's why so many of our workplaces are full of demoralized, debilitated, dehumanized people who have to grit their teeth every day just to make it to five o'clock.

I can't tell you how profound an impact it made on my own team when I just gave them space to be human. That meant, among other things, that if a sales rep was having a bad day, I didn't drop the hammer on them. Instead, I tried to figure out what was going on in their lives, gave them space to have a bad day, and tried to help out, if I could.

A little bit of genuine compassion from the sales manager goes a long way. People became more engaged at work and more committed to the mission of the company, because they didn't live in fear of being honest. The sword of Damocles wasn't looming over their heads, waiting to drop at the first sign of "personal feelings" in the workplace.

DON'T DISMISS THE NIGHTMARE

A couple of months into the global pandemic, we found ourselves struggling mightily, like a lot of business leaders, to figure out how to conduct business as usual and not just shut everything down. As I mentioned earlier, nightly emails continued to go out, as they always had, that showed the sales rankings. The longer the pandemic went on, the more I would open these emails and cringe. They seemed out of step with the reality that people were dealing with daily.

So many people were now in the red. It looked bad on the computer screen, but the email made no reference to the external global nightmare everyone was going through. Now, the leader who was sending out those emails wasn't trying to hurt anybody. He was just trying to keep everyone posted about where we stood with sales so he could help keep the ship righted and moving in a good direction.

But it felt like a perfect storm of being out of touch. If there was one thing our freaked-out team members *didn't* need to hear, it was, "Nothing to see here, nothing to worry about. Just keep selling!"

Finally, as I said, I called him and we hashed it out. We went back and forth on this topic for a while, because somehow we had to strike a balance between running a profitable business that would pay everyone's bills and expressing some empathy for struggling team members. In the end, I said, "I think if we will just take a moment as an organization to acknowledge the fear and worry people feel right now, it will go a long way."

After an hour-and-a-half discussion, he agreed. "I think I see your point," he said, "and I'm glad you spoke about this so passionately. I don't know if I would've gotten it otherwise."

The next day, rather than sending out another sales ranking email, he sent out a message of compassion in his own words.

Remember, at that time, two months into the pandemic, it was all a big mystery. Nobody knew how things were going to play out, so the message said, in part, "We're aware that there are things outside of our control in the world right now, and we want to make sure that all of your voices are heard at this time."

I was relieved. The people working for me were relieved. And the stress level of the whole organization went down. Employees felt comforted knowing that leadership was aware of their worries, sympathized, and wanted to hear from them. People were given the space to express their concerns, and as a result, they became far more engaged during a very difficult period of time.

People started saying things like, "We're going to get through this together. The company is going to make it, and we'll be okay." They began offering feedback and advice for getting through the pandemic. Team cohesion increased, while many other companies were crumbling internally.

LEARN TO CARE

Why is it that some leaders simply do not (or cannot) put themselves in their employees' shoes? Why do they seem so single-minded about performance and numbers that they act like they're oblivious to hellish conditions in the lives of their team members?

Honestly, I think some of this comes from fear. Leaders are afraid that if they show too much compassion or vulnerability, people will stop respecting them, or that they will appear weak and employees will begin taking advantage of them. They equate strong leadership with rigidity and control, not compassion and understanding, because that's how you get people to listen to you (they think).

Then again, some leaders genuinely lack empathy; some are true narcissists. But I think most leaders are just trying to keep bringing in the results—so they keep pushing, even in the face of emotional turmoil. Ironically, the hard-ass approach tends to demoralize and ultimately reduce performance, in my experience. Showing some compassion and giving people breathing room to deal with their feelings creates a more engaged workforce, and that's always better in the long run.

So, if you see someone struggling, if their performance is down one day, don't immediately pass judgment. Don't bring the hammer down. Instead, take some time to ask yourself, "What could be going on to cause this? What variable am I not aware of? What's happening in this person's world that might create this behavior?" Try to put yourself in their shoes first.

Of course, sometimes the offense is so egregious that no amount of context makes it okay. You need to have reasonable boundaries in place for employee behavior and performance. For example, you can't just let an employee steal from you. "Oh, he took a few hundred dollars out of my desk drawer? Well, he's having a bad day. His ferret got run over by an ice cream truck this morning. I'll let it slide this time."

That won't fly. But most of the time, we're talking about a dip in performance or a change in mood or some other less troubling behavior. If you don't know what could be causing it, or what factor might be influencing it, go and ask them.

When I started treating my sales reps with a bit more compassion and understanding—with healthy boundaries in place, of course—it improved their performance and sales numbers across the board.

Remember, if you're a sales manager, you were once a successful sales rep, and good salespeople know how to connect with people. You might have shut that off when you became a leader, but you used to be really curious when talking to pro-spective clients. You asked them how their day was going. You took time to talk about their personal lives. You asked them about their feelings and got to know them. You were curious!

I don't know why we stop doing that when we become sales managers, but the skill is still in there somewhere. It's time to bring it out again, only this time, instead of being curious and compassionate toward prospects, you're going to show those traits to your sales reps.

You will be absolutely astonished at how "humaning" will help you in every aspect of your business—and, quite frankly, your personal life. I recommend getting yourself some books on developing your emotional intelligence. Learn better conversa-tion skills so you can figure out where people are coming from. Develop the ability to address conflict and personal problems with empathy.

This will not only create a healthier and happier work envi-ronment, it will make your life more enjoyable overall. If you're looking for a good book on this topic, I recommend one called *Crucial Conversations: Tools for Talking When Stakes Are High*. Another good one is *Emotional Intelligence* by Daniel Goleman. I give these books to all of my new sales reps, and I've taken them to heart myself.

They are a lot more fun than reading *The Little Red Book of Sales*, I can tell you that.

Chapter Seven

MASTER OF PUPPETS

"If we inspire people, they will give us more than we asked for. If we manipulate them, they will give us exactly what we paid for."

—SIMON SINEK

No one likes to feel controlled, and your employees are not your puppets. Treating employees like you are their puppet master is the worst possible way to inspire and motivate a team.

On the other hand, people do like to be inspired and influenced. The question is, which way do you tend to lean as a leader? Do you try to control people, or do you try to influence and inspire them?

Remember the old cigar-chomping guy in the power suit? Yeah, he prefers controls. A good day at work for him is a day where he was able to get every employee to do and say exactly what he wanted.

But here's the thing: people own the ideas they create, so collaborating with your employees always creates a more engaged workforce than trying to control them. When there's a problem, work together to find solutions. Manipulation should always be an absolute *no* in leadership, and that's what you're doing when you're trying to be a puppet master.

Think about a marionette. It can dance, it can move around on stage and do all kinds of interesting-looking things, but it has no thought, no control over itself, and no will of its own. What happens when the puppeteer walks away? The marionette crashes to the ground with all of its strings and does absolutely nothing. It just lies there like dead weight.

So if you want to keep that marionette performing, you have to stick close at all times and constantly pull those strings. Is that *really* the kind of relationship you want to have with your employees? Do you want to have to worry constantly about what they do, or don't do, when you're not watching, not breathing down their necks, not pulling the strings?

Bosses go on vacation (maybe). They get sick. They have to go to conferences and meetings. If you have to constantly watch what's happening so you can control your employees and keep them dancing on the ends of their strings, you'll never have a moment's peace when you're away. You haven't influenced them. They're not inspired to keep following your example when you're not there. They're just used to being manipulated by you. Is that *really* the way you want to lead?

THE PEOPLE BUSINESS

Personally, I'm in the people business, not the manipulation business. I want to inspire and influence people, because it makes a deeper and more meaningful impact on them. What does it look like to influence instead of controlling people? First of all, you model the behavior that you want to see. Talk to sales reps the way you want them to talk to clients. Work with the same level of commitment and excellence that you want to see in their performance. That's called integrity.

Don't do things that you don't want your team members doing. One popular manipulation technique that toxic leaders love is gossip. Want to get Billy Bob to stop doing something? Well, pull him aside and gossip about how Clarence does the same stupid thing and how awful it is:

"Man, have you ever noticed how much Clarence interrupts clients during sales calls? That's so annoying."

All that does is make Billy Bob assume you also talk badly about him when he's out of the room. More than that, it creates an environment of gossip, where everyone talks badly about everyone else. No sane person wants to work in a place like that, and no one is ever going to respect a boss who always "spills the tea" about other people. They'll be guarded around you, and they will never trust you.

Influencing people is about giving ideas and perspectives, not barking orders or using threats, not manipulating or pulling strings.

KEYS TO HUMAN LEADERSHIP

If you're going to influence and inspire a team, it's important to understand what sort of outcome you're guiding them toward. This varies somewhat depending on your industry. My focus is on sales leadership, but I think there are a few principles that apply more broadly.

Ultimately, a sales leader should strive to accomplish a few key things:

1. Create a positive environment where everyone feels like they are winning.

2. Develop your team members (and yourself) to reach their (and your) potential.
3. Inspire sales reps to exceed quota without threats or toxicity.

You will accomplish all of the above better if you teach your people how to think for themselves, rather than trying to produce little automatons who just do and say what you want. Obviously, actual sales numbers are important. Companies don't grow if sales reps don't hit and exceed their numbers. However, the way you go about doing this makes a huge difference in the kind of workplace environment you create.

Remember, communication is key, so create crystal clear expectations. Don't send mixed signals to your team. Be consistent and deliver important information. Don't dilute your message with extraneous details, don't soften the central message, and make sure respect is a two-way street. You won't have to worry about trying to control people like a master of puppets if you gain their respect.

Above all, create an environment where they can thrive, and *show* them how to be successful. Now, even under the best circumstances, there are going to be times when you need to change a team member's behavior, and when that happens, embrace a "carrot and stick" approach.

CARROT AND STICK

You've probably seen the old image of the rider on top of a mule who uses a carrot on the end of a stick to keep the animal moving. There's a promise being made to the mule: "If you'll keep moving forward, you will eventually reach the carrot."

I believe the traditional leadership approach is generally based more around the "stick" than the "carrot." There's an inherent threat hovering over employees. The boss might say it explicitly or it may be implied, but it's there (and a very real threat): "Here's what I expect of you, and if you don't do it, you don't get paid and may get fired." In other words, "Keep moving toward the carrot, or I'll whack you with the stick."

You *can* lead that way. A lot of people certainly do. People need to get paid. They've got bills. So they'll try to do what you expect of them. However, they'll never go above and beyond, and they'll never be truly engaged at work. Why would they? They don't like you. They don't respect you. All they care about is making sure they get their paycheck. You've taught them to relate to you in that way. They need to eat that carrot to stay alive, and they really don't want to get whacked with the stick.

If you really want engaged people who *like* coming to work, respect you, and want to do their absolute best, it's better to lean more on the "carrot" than the "stick." Instead of creating some looming threat that hovers in the air over them as they work, try to help your people see and understand the good outcomes they will achieve from performing at a high level.

This is super easy to do in sales. The "carrot" of performing at a high level is more sales, more commissions, more money. You shouldn't need to threaten anyone. Inspire them to catch a vision of what they might accomplish and how it's going to make everything better!

Now, to be clear, there are exceptions. There are times when you have to use the stick and not the carrot, but only when someone breaks a cardinal rule. If you catch an employee lying, cheating, or stealing, then "inspiration" is probably not a strong enough response. But that's why organizations set rules and create guidebooks.

Other than those rare instances, I've found that leaders are most effective when they focus on communicating the good outcome rather than using threats or manipulation. Whether you're dealing with performance, self-development, or a change in behavior or attitude, if you will inspire and influence your people by trying to give them a vision of the outcome they can achieve, you will make a more significant impact. When someone makes a change because they've been inspired, rather than threatened or controlled, they are more likely to fully embrace the change, even when you're not around.

Now, the "carrot" that you use—the good outcome you point them toward—will vary depending on the situation, as well as what drives a particular individual. However, almost everyone likes money, so you can't go wrong helping them catch a vision of greater commissions, a bigger end-of-the-year bonus, or a raise.

If you're working for a nonprofit and you can't really use money as a driver, maybe you can use recognition or some form of public acknowledgment like an awards banquet or special ceremony. Whatever the case, when you're trying to get someone to change a behavior, the idea is to point them to the potential good outcome of making the change, rather than simply trying to pull the marionette strings harder and force them to dance.

In my experience, a good leader will use a harsh approach about 5 percent of the time, and only to deal with serious rule violations. If you find yourself having to threaten employees more often than that, something is really wrong with your company culture or workplace environment. If you keep having to pull out the proverbial stick and start playing whack-a-mole, then either your leadership style is toxic or you need to start rooting out some deeper problems in your organization.

No workplace should look like that. The whole "carrot and stick" analogy—which I've twisted and abused in this chapter—originally referred to a kinder and gentler way of getting a stubborn animal to do what you want. Tie a carrot on a string to the end of a stick, hold it in front of the animal, and entice the animal to keep moving forward with the promise of eating the carrot. That's a lot nicer than whipping the hell out of the animal.

Hopefully, you eventually let the poor animal eat the carrot. The same with your employees. Keep them moving forward—performing well and doing the right thing—by constantly sharing the good outcomes that they will achieve, but then help them actually achieve those outcomes. Otherwise, you're just making empty promises, and people will eventually see right through you.

TELLING VS. TEACHING

My father was an undercover vice cop. You might think that would make him a tough-as-nails parent, but he actually gave me quite a bit of latitude. When friends would find out his profession, they would say things like, "Wow, he must be really strict." On the contrary, his parenting approach was all about talking to me, sharing wisdom, and encouraging me.

As he later explained to me, "In order for you to survive in this world when I'm not looking, I want you to learn how to make smart choices on your own. After all, some of those choices may be life or death." He knew a harsh parenting style would only make me obey out of fear, and possibly push me to rebel when he wasn't around, but if he could inspire me and share his knowledge, I might take his teaching to heart and apply it to my life. And I like to think I did just that.

Obviously, sales and business aren't usually life or death, though it may feel like that sometimes. However, the point is the same. As leaders, we need our people to be willing and able to make smart choices even when we're not around. We need them to become critical thinkers who look beyond some immediate threat to their livelihood and find a more compelling motivation.

"Could I be closing more sales if I invested a little more time in making the prospect feel understood? Will I open up more career advancement opportunities if I go beyond minimum requirements?" And so on.

In a sense, being a leader is a lot like being a parent. If you have to put baby cams all over your house when you go away for the weekend so your seventeen-year-old daughter doesn't throw a party and destroy the house, you probably went wrong somewhere in parenting her. You know you've truly raised your kids well when you can trust them to make difficult decisions and act with integrity even when you're not around.

You'll get that same kind of performance integrity from employees far more often when you stop trying to be a puppet master and focus on inspiring and influencing them instead. Point them toward the good outcomes that you want them to achieve, teach them to think critically, and model the kind of behavior you want to see. That's how you get better performance on a more consistent basis.

Chapter Eight

GROUND CONTROL TO MANAGER [INSERT YOUR NAME]

"Proud people breed sad sorrows for themselves."

—EMILY BRONTË

Highly successful people on a sales team, even leaders, can fall prey to a level of hubris that is unmeasurable. If you've been around sales long enough, you've seen it happen. One insufferable person who is full of themselves can wreak havoc on team cohesion and company culture, so how do you keep yourself and your team grounded?

Since you're reading this book, chances are you've already found yourself in a place where you're no longer kicking ass. You're looking for a bit of help with leadership because things are no longer going smoothly for you. Maybe you've already had a big dose of humility that has knocked your pride down a few pegs. Hey, that's not a bad thing, especially if it leads to some wisdom.

Discovering what it's like to no longer be on top is one of the best things that can happen to a super successful person, because a bit of humility will make you a more empathetic leader. If you just won an award or accomplished some amazing thing, or everyone's praising you, there's nothing wrong with enjoying it. I think it's healthy to cherish our accomplishments and acclaim, but sometimes we need to check ourselves.

The ego can get inflated. When that happens, you need to remind yourself that success is fleeting, and all kinds of things can get in the way. The people who have the most trouble making the transition into leadership tend to be those whose entire identity is based on their accomplishments. Effective leaders have to stay humble.

Unfortunately, we heap praise on the really good sales reps. We give them awards, bonuses, and "attaboys" of one kind or another to encourage them to keep breaking records, and to encourage others to follow their example. Over time, they get used to being praised, but then they get moved into leadership and the inflated ego goes with them. They forget that they're not out there saving lives.

Companies and coworkers tolerate an egotistical sales rep because they bring in money, but no one—*no one*—likes an egotistical boss. If you're now in leadership, you need to bring yourself back down to earth or you're not going to thrive in your new position. Maybe you don't need to post all of your old sales awards all over your office anymore.

Just remember, your success in sales was partly down to luck. You lucked into a job where your personality or talents were a benefit. You were lucky that you didn't encounter any career-derailing calamities, as some people have. Hard work helps, talent helps, but luck plays a big role in any successful person's life. And luck can change without a moment's notice. Never forget that.

Don't kick anyone while they're down, because you might be down tomorrow. Your luck can change, no matter how awesome you think you are. Keep your success in the right perspective.

REMEMBER WHERE YOU CAME FROM

If you're riding high on your sales success and all of your awards, try to remember where you came from. And remember how quickly everything can be taken away.

Personally, I am not a college graduate. I spent my formative early adult years as a waitress. In fact, I didn't even start my first sales job until I was in my thirties. While I thrived as a sales rep, I can still remember what it felt like to come home from working as a waitress, filthy, stinking like the Olive Garden. I would stumble through the door and collapse on the couch. It was a tough job, and it didn't pay a lot of money. I was counting change.

Any time the ego tries to rear its head, it's important for me to remember those days. It helps bring me back down to earth. Most of us have had crappy jobs. If you need to, use your memory of that time as a way to keep yourself humble.

PRACTICE GRATITUDE

Another way I keep myself humble is to practice gratitude. Every day, I try to write down five things I'm grateful for in a little journal. Not only does this keep my mind focused on the things that make me happy, but it also helps me deal with challenges. When a problem comes my way, I think about all of the wonderful things in my life so the problem doesn't consume my mind.

Not only that, practicing gratitude helps keep me grounded

because a lot of the things on my list have to do with other people—things others have done for me, ways they've helped me, the blessing of their relationships in my life, and so on.

This is such a powerful practice that I've often recommended it to my sales reps. I don't require it of them, of course. Making it obligatory would turn it into drudgery, but I have the occasional impromptu meetings where everyone has a chance to share what they're grateful for, if they want to. During those meetings, I might share a story or read an article on gratitude, then "open the floor" if others want to share.

Often, I'll open these meetings by saying something like, "Hey, guys, we don't have a lot on our agenda today, so instead, let's just talk about what's going on in our lives. Specifically, what's going right? It's easy to talk about what's going wrong, but what are some good things happening?"

Sometimes, when we practice gratitude, we start with materialistic things: "I have a Mercedes. I own five Louis Vuitton bags." But if we keep at it, if we list enough things, eventually we get to the stuff that really matters, stuff like, "I'm healthy. My parents are still here. I have great friends." You can only list so much materialistic crap before you have to dig a little deeper into the real good stuff, like relationships, experiences, opportunities, acts of kindness, and so on.

And don't just write this stuff down. Talk about it. Make it a habit to mention it in conversation around the office. Not just what you're grateful for, but how lucky you are. If you regularly talk about how lucky you've been in your career, it'll make you seem a lot less egocentric. It removes some of that superiority complex that might have served you well in sales but makes you insufferable as a leader.

I've shared my situation with you already. I've been through multiple brain surgeries and a long, grueling recovery. As a result of everything, I also have occasional seizures, which can hit without warning. And yet, despite everything I've been through in the last few years, I feel so incredibly lucky.

According to my doctor, some people who have seizures after a brain tumor get them so bad that they can't even get out of bed. And here I am, still working, still leading my team, and even writing this book. Not too shabby. I think about this a lot, and I talk about it. And when I consider how lucky I've been, I also remember all the people—friends, family, medical professionals, and so many coworkers—who have helped me, supported me, asked how I was doing, and accommodated me along the way.

How could I not stay humble? So I've made sure to thank them. When people show sincere interest in how I'm doing, it's my pleasure to share all the good news about how far I've come, how much better I'm feeling, and all the great things that have happened.

It would be easy to throw a pity party about my situation, but that doesn't solve anything either. Now, I don't want to be fake and pretend like I'm doing better than I really am, but I get to choose what I focus on. By focusing on gratitude, I stay both humble and hopeful, and that's a great place for a leader to be.

Neither an inflated ego nor self-pity makes for effective leadership. Stay grateful. Stay humble. Remind yourself how lucky you've been. Instill this attitude into your team and make it a part of your workplace.

The next time you have a team meeting, spend some time sharing with one another about how grateful you are. Share it with your own boss, as well. I promise, you will be amazed at the impact this has on you as a leader, as well as the impact it makes on your team.

No one responds well to a cocky egomaniac, but people feel

inspired by a grounded, hopeful, and grateful leader who isn't afraid to talk about how blessed and lucky they've been.

HERDING CATS/ BULLS ON PARADE

"I would like to see anyone—prophet, king, or God—convince a thousand cats to do the same thing at the same time."

—NEIL GAIMAN

I own two Bengal cats and a Russian blue. The Russian blue is just a normal cat, an ordinary lazy little creature, but the Bengals are nuts. They are like cats cranked up to eleven. A cursory Google search on the breed presented me with this list of "Bengal Behavior Concerns":

- Highly active and full of energy
- Very demanding
- Potential challenging temperament[2]

---

2   "Bengal," VCA Animal Hospitals, https://vcahospitals.com/know-your-pet/cat-breeds/bengal (accessed April 25, 2024).

Yeah, all of that rings true. They can be a lot of fun, but they're super inquisitive. They get into everything. They become bored easily, and if not properly stimulated, they can start bouncing off the walls.

Can you imagine trying to herd a bunch of Bengal cats? It would be an exercise in futility. You might as well try to herd a whirlwind.

Sometimes, it feels kind of the same trying to manage a sales team, and *especially* your superstar reps. Sales tends to attract a certain kind of personality, an energetic and curious personality that needs constant stimulation. One of the big struggles as a leader is trying to think and move quickly enough to keep these people engaged and interested in what they're supposed to be doing. You can shout, "Pay attention! Focus! Concentrate!" until you're red in the face, and they'll still be bouncing off the walls.

Other times, they can feel more like bulls on parade—not unlike the running of the bulls in Pamplona. Just a bunch of big, aggressive animals who are trampling everything in their path and leaving destruction in their wake. You want them to be careful, be smart, and deal with prospects and clients with wisdom and care, but they want to rush ahead as fast as they can.

DOING THINGS THEIR OWN WAY

Now, to be clear, I'm not putting down Bengal cats (or bulls, for that matter). I love my pets, and Bengals are very special animals.

In a similar way, superstar salespeople are also very special. Just like Bengals, they're going to do what they want when they want. That's why superstar sales reps sometimes set a bad example for other salespeople, even though they're hitting great numbers. They don't always follow the rules. They want to do things their own way, and while they might have the talent or the natural personality to make it work for them, it's not necessarily effective for other reps to follow their lead.

It makes sense that many reps would be this way. After all, why do a lot of people go into sales? Because they want to be in charge of their destiny. They don't want to work a regular hourly job with hourly wages. They'd rather have a job where their income depends on their own tenacity, grit, and determination, and sales gives them that.

This can be a good thing. The superstar sales reps don't give up. They keep pushing forward to sell more, achieve more, earn more. On the other hand, if you try to get them to do something that's boring, or that doesn't clearly advance their own agenda, they're going to start clawing the proverbial furniture.

If you're a new sales leader, there's one very important thing that you need to remember: a great sales rep still needs constant development!

Just because they have a knack for winning over prospects and getting them to sign on the dotted line doesn't mean there aren't other areas of their job that they still need to work on. They may get so bored doing paperwork that they want to poke themselves in the eye, but they still need to learn how to get it done in a timely manner. Their sales record might be impressive, but they still struggle to show up to team meetings on time.

You have to find ways to harness some of that boundless energy they have for sales and channel it into the other important parts of the job that they don't love. Use the carrot and stick, inspire and influence, whatever you have to do, to help them learn how to focus on those tasks. They can get better at it. Someday, with consistent leadership, they'll learn to show up on time to meetings or sit down and do all of that paperwork without going nuts.

Remember, people like these want to be in charge of their own destiny, and they are motivated by money and recognition. That's why they went into sales. They crave constant adrenaline and having their egos fed. If you get in their way, they will trample you to get to the prize. It's tempting for leaders to let them go wild because they bring in sales, but you're doing them a favor if you spend some time trying to hone and improve those weak areas.

Even a Bengal cat can have its behavior modified. You can work on the cat's destructive tendencies and traits with a bit of patience, a carrot-and-stick approach, and all of the other things we've talked about. It takes time, consistency, and integrity on your part, but it's worth the effort.

You'll build team cohesion, of course, but you'll also set those superstar sales reps up for success when they finally climb the ladder into leadership. So herd the cats. It's not impossible. Be patient and persistent. It's good for them, and good for all the other cats.

LEARN ABOUT PEOPLE

A good leader is a good coach, and a good coach always learns the backgrounds, blind spots, and "whys" of their team members. If you do this well, it becomes a whole lot easier to modify some of the negative behaviors that get them in trouble.

This starts during the interview process. We'll talk about hiring in an upcoming chapter, but for now, it's important to remember that every human being has some good traits and bad traits. If you can figure out what makes someone tick, it's a whole lot easier to inspire and influence them in the right direction. The best way to start learning these things is to simply ask people.

Recognize that every member of your team and every potential hire is an individual, a unique human being, not an archetype. So just ask. I know some people struggle to ask old-school questions like, "What are your biggest challenges? What do you see as your strengths and weaknesses?" But there is value in these questions.

Still, you have to push past the cliché answers like, "I'm a perfectionist. I'm a workaholic. I try too hard sometimes." That's not what you're looking for, so probe for meaningful answers: "Tell me about a time that your temper, or some other area of challenge, got you in trouble." The more you get to know them, the easier it becomes to guide them, so start getting to know them from the first conversation.

At the same time, you need to let people know right up front what you want from them. Don't be afraid to warn them that this is a high-pressure job—within reason, of course. You don't need to oversell how hard a job is.

If people understand what's going to be expected of them, and if they get a sense of how tough the job can be, bad candidates will tend to catch themselves. If you do end up hiring someone, that honest conversation in the beginning will make it a lot easier to have honest conversations in the future. Later on, when you see that new sales rep struggling in some area, you can say, "Do you remember what we talked about before? How you have a hard time keeping your emotions in check when a big sale is on the line? If you think someone is messing it up for you, you tend to overreact. Well, I think that's happening again, so how can I help you?"

You can't give honest feedback like that if you don't really know someone, understand what makes them tick, and become aware of their strengths and weaknesses. That open conversation right in the beginning, when you ask them a lot of situational questions about their last job, sets the standard. And if they get comfortable talking to you about areas of needed growth, they will often begin to self-develop in those areas.

Also, if you need to confront them about something they've done, if they're going out of bounds in some area, it won't be as much of a confrontation. You already know them, so instead of pointing the finger and accusing, you can simply continue the conversation.

"Hey, you did that thing again. You know, the thing we've talked about that's a struggle for you. What was going on this time? And what can we do to support you and help you grow in that area?"

Everyone's going to make mistakes. There's no reason to go nuclear when good old Billy Bob is late on his paperwork again. You know it's an area of struggle for him, so address it honestly, with compassion, but push toward a solution.

Of course, *you* are going to make mistakes, too. Leaders have their areas of weakness as well, and when you mess up, you need to be honest about it. Model the behaviors of self-reflection and introspection. You want your employees to be honest with you about their areas of struggle, so be honest with them when you struggle. Give yourself a break just like you give them a break, apologize, and then move on.

Now, there's a healthy balance here. You need to address problems and not merely gloss over them. You don't want to create an environment where a sales rep says, "That's just how I am," when they mess up. "Hey, I'm just not really good with paperwork, and I never will be. You already know that." That's not acceptable. Awareness of a weakness should lead to a conversation about development and improvement: "What can we do to help in this area?"

Also, as in any job, there are going to be some non-negotiables, where you can't allow someone to simply call it an area of weakness. "Sorry, boss, I lied about my sales numbers. That's just something I struggle with. I'll try to do better next time and put the real numbers down." That's obviously not going to fly.

LAY THE RIGHT FOUNDATION

So is it possible to herd a bunch of cats? As it turns out, yes, as long as you establish the right relationship with them from the beginning. Get to know them. Learn what makes them tick. Understand where they struggle. Create an environment of open and honest discussion from day one, so that when they knock a lamp off the table, you can talk about it—because you've already talked about it!

Set up the relationship from the beginning. Clarify the non-negotiables and encourage self-development. Learn what they like and don't like. Then keep that relationship going. Model some of these self-reflective behaviors. Show them that you're also trying to grow and improve in your own areas of weakness. If you do this well, you won't be constantly chasing people and trying to put out fires.

To continue the relationship, schedule regular one-on-one meetings with each of your team members, and make sure those meetings *aren't* just about the numbers. All too often, especially in sales, every meeting is nothing more than reviewing numbers, reviewing pipelines. From time to time, you need to sit down and talk about everything else besides the numbers.

Start these conversations by building genuine rapport:

"Hey, how are you doing today? What's going on? What's new?"

Compliment them on something good that they've done—

and genuinely mean it! Yes, that's going to require a bit of preparation on your part, so before you meet with them, figure out some awesome thing they've done recently, even if it's small. Make a note to bring it up during the meeting.

And, hey, you don't have to wait for a meeting to build rapport. I've made it a habit to pick up the phone sometimes and just call people to check on them: "Hey, how are things going? I haven't talked to you one-on-one in a couple of days. How's that big sale you were working on? Is there anything I can do right now to support you?" And so on.

In other words, check in with people on a regular basis, not just during a scheduled meeting, and create space for the relationship. If you work in person, stop by from time to time and ask how they're doing, offer some help. If it's not in person, an occasional unscheduled phone call works just fine. In my experience, the vast majority of reps are going to be excited that you called, especially if you establish that you genuinely care about their well-being.

If you create space for the relationship, the business is going to flow more naturally. Dealing with problems will become easier. In short, everything will go just a little smoother, so it's worth the time and effort.

CATS AND BULLS CAN SELL

Ultimately, those same frustrating qualities that make leading sales reps feel like either herding cats or dealing with bulls on parade also make them good at selling. Cats are predators. They need to hunt, and you can hone their hunting ability in such a way that they're going after the right things and not leaving a wake of destruction around the home.

I first dealt with this as a new leader at Paychex. I had a superstar rep who was amazing at selling and also a wonderful person. However, he drove all of our service operations managers crazy. Not intentionally, mind you. Rather, his personality was just so different from theirs. He was a wild ball of energy, and they were steady. It was a struggle trying to make them all get along.

Finally, I had an epiphany. I put myself in the rep's shoes and tried to see things from his perspective. It takes a particular kind of personality to feel comfortable cold calling prospects and trying to get them interested in setting an appointment, then grabbing their attention during that meeting and trying to convince them to open up and share with you—knowing all the while that they might reject you at any point.

Even a superstar rep has to deal with ten or twenty rejections a day, depending on the industry and what they're selling. Somehow, they have to just absorb these rejections and keep plugging away, keep trying to win people over. It takes an intense personality to *enjoy* doing this day after day, and that intensity is going to rub someone with a steadier and calmer personality the wrong way from time to time.

I knew I had to help my service managers understand where the annoying superstar rep was coming from, while also encouraging the rep to make some adjustments in his approach that would smooth a few of those rough edges. Fortunately, I'm a bit of a hybrid myself. I'm usually steady and stable, but I'm not entirely conflict avoidant. I pick and choose the hills I'm willing to die on.

However, reps like this guy are often in fight mode from the minute they wake up, check their emails, and start planning their day. As soon as the sun is up, they're thinking about the problems they'll have to overcome, the things that are going to get in the way, and the many, many challenges they're going to tackle head on. Often, fight mode comes to them naturally, and they have a hard time cranking the dial down. They can get a lot better at it over time if you coach them, but there's going to be tension—it's practically unavoidable.

We sell products that get serviced, so we have service managers. The kinds of people who make good service managers are very, very different from the kind who make great sales reps. Somehow, they have to learn to get along. A good starting point is getting them to understand each other.

When there's conflict, I recommend speaking to your sales rep.

"Hey, would you want to do the job of these service managers?"

"No way, boss. I would hate that job."

"But we need service managers, don't we? They keep our clients happy, and that's good for us."

"Yeah, that's true. It's very good for us."

"Okay, then, would you take it easy on them? Lower the porcupine quills when you're dealing with them, because we need them. Can you do that?"

"Sure thing, boss."

Through regular conversations like these, you can help that intense sales rep understand the value of service managers (and any others they tend to rub the wrong way). Sales reps sometimes think that their position is the only one that really matters—after all, they're the ones actually making sales and bringing in money. Help them understand that all roles are important. Humanize the service managers and others. At the same time, you can help the service manager understand the sales rep's intensity.

Bad leaders look the other way. "As long as people are making sales, who cares that they annoy people? Those service managers are only employed because my reps are closing deals." That's no way to create a strong, cohesive team or a healthy workplace. That's a good way to drive off talent and create dysfunction.

Yes, cats and bulls can sell, but they have to get along with the other animals on the farm. Every animal is there for a reason.

TELL ME MORE

If you're struggling to get through to some of your sales reps, if they seem constantly on the verge of being out of control, you probably need to do a bit more relationship work. Strive a little harder to understand their "why," as good old Simon Sinek likes to say. If you understand what drives someone, what they're working toward, their real motivation, then it becomes a lot easier to redirect them when there's trouble.

You can ask them about it during your regular meetings. "What does success mean to you? What are you really working toward?"

Maybe they're trying to save up so they can build a pool, or send their daughter to a good college, or retire early with dignity. Maybe they just want to make a ton of money so they can live the good life. Or they crave financial stability. Or they're trying to surpass someone's expectations.

Whatever the case, talk about it. Create space for developing the relationship and show genuine interest in them as people. Once you know what motivates someone, you can bring them back to the motivation when they get a little off track—just like I might use a cat treat to get one of my Bengals to stop climbing on the curtains. When you talk to a rep about their "why," don't accept a shallow answer. Dig a little deeper. "Tell me more. Why do you work so hard? What do you really want to achieve?"

"Hey, remember when you told me about that thing you want so badly? Well, if you keep going off track in this area here, you're going to make it harder to reach your goal."

Relate performance issues back to their "why," and they will not only respond better to correction, they will appreciate you for it.

"You've got to get along with the service managers, because they're going to help us create loyal customers who will buy from us again. And those client relationships are what will help you make the money you need to retire, so let's try to get along with them, okay?"

If your sales reps have restless energy, channel it productively. My Bengal cats have this giant hamster wheel, about three and a half feet tall, and when they're worked up, they'll get on the wheel and run until they're exhausted. It's better than letting them race all around the house and tear things up. Sometimes, they run so fast, they fly off the wheel and crash land on the carpet.

That kind of feels like a good metaphor for Salesforce. But this restless energy is what keeps a sales rep going in the face of rejection. They need it, and we all need them. Even so, you can indeed herd cats with a bit of patience in building the relationship, finding out what motivates them, and encouraging them to broaden their perspective of others.

······· *Chapter Ten* ·······

THE HALO EFFECT

"Overworking is the Black Plague of the 21st Century."

—RICHIE NORTON

Let's just say it. The sales world is full of sleep-deprived sales leaders who don't spend enough time with their families, don't take enough vacations, work late hours, and frequently come to work when they're sick.

Okay, now let's say it more professionally. It's not uncommon for people in leadership to have to check themselves about their own work–life balance. Sales managers, in particular, take on a lot and have a lot of expectations placed upon them. Things can easily get out of whack as you try to juggle all of your responsibilities. So many sales managers are running in the red to stay on top of it all, but you can't run in the red forever.

As I mentioned before, my dad was a police officer, and he used to tell me about something called the "halo effect." This is his definition of it, not perhaps the technical definition. According to my father's understanding, the halo effect refers to how we judge people based on them possessing certain traits. Police officers in my dad's department always tried to exhibit these behaviors so that people would respond more positively to them.

"We have to model certain behaviors," he said, "if we want to earn the community's respect."

This, of course, applies to leaders in all industries. If you want to earn the respect of your team, you have to model the behaviors that they view as "good leadership traits."

However, that's not actually what I want to talk about. I want to talk about something that leaders do *in reverse*. You see, leaders tend to practice a version of the halo effect where they look for certain traits of their own in their team members. And sometimes, those traits are toxic.

One of the most common examples is this tendency to overwork. As I said, leaders often run in the red. They're workaholics who can easily spend eighty hours a week in the office. They skip vacations. Sometimes they work on the weekends. They stay late every night. None of that is healthy, of course. None of it. The real problem comes when those workaholic leaders expect their sales reps to do the same thing.

"I work eighty hours a week because I care about this job," they think, "and if my sales reps really cared, they'd work long hours, too. They'd stay after five o'clock, they'd come in on Saturday. Instead, it's like they can't wait to get out of here!" They get annoyed when people plan vacations and then actually take them, or won't work weekends and instead go to their kid's soccer game. The audacity!

UNHEALTHY LEADERS CREATE UNHEALTHY WORKPLACES

Forget about the horrible effect this has on your employees for a minute. It's bad for you, too! A good leader must create balance in their lives. I know it's tempting to tell your people,

"I'm always available. Contact me about work-related issues any time of the day or night." But you're not doing yourself any favors, and you're not doing them any favors.

You're going to burn yourself out like that. Furthermore, if you feel like you always have to be around because you always need to handle any issues that arise, you are not teaching your employees to think for themselves. Take the damn vacation! Get someone to cover for you. People have to learn how to perform and keep the gears in the machine spinning when you're not around. They'll never learn if you're always there, so go home! Go home to your spouse, to your kids, to your hobbies. Go home, eat a nice meal, and go to bed at a reasonable hour.

When you work constantly, you create the expectation that everyone is supposed to work eighty hours a week. Employees get scared to take vacations because you never take them. They're afraid to stay home when they're sick because you drag yourself into the office even when you're coughing, sweating, and shaking like a leaf in a hurricane. This creates a deeply unhealthy environment—a workplace where people burn out, where turnover is high, where no one likes anyone.

But maybe you're not even aware that you work too much. Maybe it all feels routine to you. So here's a little test. Go ask your family if they think you work too much. They can see what you don't see. "Yeah, Mom, it would be nice if you were here on Saturday and Sunday. I wish we could go to the beach this summer. I wish you came to my games, went to the movies with us, or took us places sometimes."

I know you're probably not working too much just for the hell of it. You're trying to help your team and your company do well, and people rely on you so much. You want to keep your reps performing at a high level, keep those numbers up, and you're afraid it won't happen if you're not always working.

But here's the thing: If you were less of a puppet master and more of an influencer, the impact of your leadership would stick when you're not around. If you truly inspired your people, they would rise to the occasion when you're out of town, or home on the weekend, or taking a sick day. If you have to constantly run all-nighters, you're probably not influencing or inspiring your people. You're still just pulling strings.

TAKE A BREAK

You have placed unhealthy expectations on yourself, and you're placing those same unhealthy expectations on your team members. Don't push your workaholism on your sales reps. Just because it's your jam to work twelve hours a day doesn't mean anyone should have to do it. If you're not going to take care of yourself, at least let other people live healthy balanced lives.

Yes, in any sales environment, you have to maintain a funnel of sales activity, but a good leader helps their people plan leisure activities so they can enjoy some time away. Help them relax and recharge by making sure people cover for them. If you do this well, they'll be able to come back without starting from zero. Coordinate things like vacations and time off with various team members so everyone is getting plenty of rest without bringing your sales machine to a grinding halt.

As leaders, we have to stop pushing people to adopt our unhealthy personal working habits. Better yet, let's fix our own unhealthy habits so we're not racing toward an early stress-induced grave. Create a workplace where you can trust people to cover for you, to pick up the slack when you're not in the office, where all the marionettes aren't going to come crashing down onto the stage just because you took a three-day weekend to celebrate your wedding anniversary.

Everyone in every profession needs time off to recharge. Emergency room doctors take time off. Paramedics take time off. Police officers like my father take time off. Yes, there's a unique aspect of sales because you need to keep your pipeline open. It's not like a light switch you can turn on and off. However, if you know you're going on vacation, you can get people to cover for you.

There are a lot of strategies you can use to make sure the pipeline keeps going even when people are gone, so that when someone goes on vacation, they're not still thinking about work constantly or coming back to find that they've lost all momentum. A healthy workplace can handle this. Model it in your own life, so your sales reps will feel safe to do the same.

Strike a healthy balance for your own sake, too. You need time to recharge. You need time with family. You need to spend a week on the beach from time to time. Do it, before you burn out and burn your reps out. Straighten up that crooked halo and model healthy behavior.

Chapter Eleven

SPEED DATING

"Time spent on hiring is time well spent."

—ROBERT HALF

One of the biggest new responsibilities you gain as a leader is the ability to hire people, but just because you now have the power doesn't mean you have any idea how to use it. If you're not thoughtful and incredibly careful about who you hire, you can introduce chaos into an otherwise functional workplace.

Have you ever seen the show *90-Day Fiancé*? Actually, it's an entire franchise of shows built around the premise that couples meet each other for the first time and then marry within ninety days of that first meeting. Do you know the success rate of those marriages? Some of the shows in the franchise have a success rate as low as 29 percent.[3] Others have been more successful, but even if they meet the national divorce rate of 40 percent, that's not the kind of success rate you want to see in your hiring.

---

3   Maggie Mead, "90 Day Fiancé Shows Ranked By Relationship Success Rate," ScreenRant (April 2, 2022), https://screenrant.com/90-day-fiance-ranked-relationship-success-rate-together.

It's amazing to me how many people will go through a hiring process and get offered a job without ever being told *why* they were hired. It's just a handshake and, "We'd like to extend you an offer to come on board," without any discussion.

"Why did you pick me? What was so special about me?" Nothing like that. Just an offer. So the new employee doesn't know what to look for, what they really have to offer, or why they're a good fit. It's just a toss of the dice. "I guess I'll accept the offer and hope it works out."

On the other side, leaders tend to hire people who look just like them. This time, I'm not necessarily talking about gender, race, sexual orientation, or things like that. I mean personality traits. A leader will think, "Oh, I like this guy. He's a fast talker like me. He reminds me of myself when I was a sales rep. I did well, so he'll probably do well."

But maybe what you were like as a young, hungry sales rep isn't what the company needs right now. Maybe it's no longer a good fit the way it was fifteen years ago. Maybe there are other non-negotiables, values, and qualities that are more important than what you had to offer back in the day.

Instead of hiring someone because you feel some personal kinship with them, you should be looking for more important qualities. What are those qualities?

THE QUALITIES OF A GOOD HIRE

First, I think it's incredibly important, especially when you're hiring a sales rep, that they have transferable skills. For example, if you're hiring someone to be a fully outside sales rep—meaning no upselling—then you need someone who has incredible cold-calling skills.

If you need a sales rep who's going to manage a book of

business, then you need someone who is skilled at building relationships and taking care of clients, who will fix their problems and keep them with the company.

Some sales reps work better alone and prefer it that way, so if it's a position where they need to work with other sales partners, they're probably not a good fit. If they don't play nicely with other children in the sandbox, don't bring them on board unless it's a fully solo sales position.

In other words, hire for their skills and their fit, not because they remind you of yourself or have certain personality traits that you like. That candidate you really liked? You won't like him so much, no matter how much he reminds you of yourself, when he starts creating chaos on your team. You don't want to learn the hard way that someone's a bad fit after they're already on the job.

To that end, at Paychex, our first conversation with a candidate during the interview process is always about getting to know the person better. We ask questions like, "What are you looking for? Why are you in the marketplace looking for a job? What do you hope to achieve? What matters most to you?"

At the same time, while I'm getting to know someone during the first meeting, I also want to see if they are able to ask me questions as well, so I encourage them to interview me back. After all, they're going to be talking to prospects and clients quite a bit. They need to demonstrate that they can keep a conversation going.

This makes our hiring process longer because we're essentially vetting each other, but it's worth it. In fact, to bring a little levity to the proceeding, I usually ask the candidate, "Have you ever bought a pair of shoes that didn't fit?"

Most of the time they say yes.

Then I ask, "How long did you wear those shoes?"

"Not long," they'll say.

"Isn't it better to try the shoes on at the store before you buy them? The same with hiring for a job, except it's a lot worse to match the wrong person with the wrong position than to buy a pair of ill-fitting shoes. You want to make sure the job is a good fit, and I want to make sure you are a good fit. That's why we both need to interview one another."

The cost in extra time that comes from a longer hiring process is far less than the cost of a high turnover rate. Beyond the hard dollar cost of constantly trying to replace sales reps and bring new people up to speed, there's the morale cost of a workplace where people are constantly leaving or being fired.

When your sales reps think you can't pick talent, they're going to lose a lot of respect for you. "This idiot keeps hiring losers!" That's going to make them question whether or not they're at the right place. "Do I want to keep working for this fool? We lose talent every week." Even if they don't leave, they're probably not going to be fully engaged, giving their all, because they don't fully believe in you.

Let me be as clear on this issue as I can be. It is *extremely* important that you are discerning when it comes to hiring. Everyone is counting on you not to wreck the place by bringing in the wrong person.

SHADOW DAY

Sometimes we make mistakes. Look, a sociopath can give a good interview. Some candidates hide aspects of themselves that only become clear once they've been on the job for a while. To avoid that, I'll have a trusted sales rep shadow a new employee for a day and observe them. In a remote job, they will listen to sales calls on Zoom or WebEx.

The person who does this doesn't have to be your number one rep, as long as they're a good, solid performing rep who is willing to do it. Afterward, the rep can come to you and tell you how it went. Maybe they'll say, "I took this candidate on a couple of sales calls, but then we went to lunch, and you should've seen how they treated the waitress! We do not want this person on our team."

Their goal is to see if there are any red flags or chinks in the armor, stuff that slipped through the interview process. A candidate will sometimes tell you what you want to hear, but once they're in the job, the real person starts showing up. Other times, the new employee experiences what the job is *really* like, and they remove themselves. "Oh, I didn't know it was going to be like this. I know you told me during the hiring process, but the reality is too intense for me."

Either way, you save yourself, the new employee, and the rest of the team a lot of heartache if you part ways early.

Avoid this if you can. Try to catch problems and "bad fit" during the interviewing process. To do that, I'll often have a peer come in and interview a candidate after me, because I know I have some unconscious biases that might make me overlook important details.

By the way, when it comes to all of these additional steps, I always let a candidate know up front what the interview process will look like. First of all, it's the decent thing to do. Second, I find that sometimes they get excited because they're going to get a better look at what the job entails. They'll have a clear view of what they're potentially stepping into. Also, it helps them trust the process because they can see you're not rushing it. When you finally make that offer, they'll understand why you chose them.

A PIPELINE OF CANDIDATES

When you're a sales rep, you don't count on one single client to make your monthly quota. Instead, you try to have a variety of people you're working with who are at all stages of your sales funnel, because timing is important. A single client can easily drop off the face of the earth, even if you do everything right.

That one client you were counting on to make a big sale for the month might back out at the last minute over a personal matter. You just never know. A single sale can always fall apart, and clients can leave for all kinds of reasons.

In a similar way, you can't assume that your current roster of sales reps will never change. You can't depend on a select few superstar salespeople to keep your team going because you never know when a rep might leave. Even if you create a beautiful, harmonious workplace, people are still going to leave sometimes, possibly when you least expect it.

Therefore, just as you have a pipeline of clients that is always moving, you need to create a pipeline of candidates so you always know where to turn when you need to fill a role. Some of the people in your pipeline might already be inside the company, working in different roles. You should also regularly attend job fairs so you can meet people. Use LinkedIn to regularly promote your business.

Make regular LinkedIn posts about what's special at your company, why you're relevant, why you're industry leaders, and so on, so you attract potential candidates. You want people reading your articles and reaching out. When used correctly, LinkedIn is a powerful tool for maintaining a pipeline of potential candidates.

Maintain a list of names so that when a rep leaves, you know exactly who you're going to reach out to and say, "Hey, an opportunity just opened up on my awesome team! Are you interested in the position?"

YOUR MOST IMPORTANT DECISION

Your hiring decisions will be among the most impactful decisions you make as a leader, so your hiring process needs to be thoughtful and thorough, both for you and for the candidate. Make sure the shoes fit before you take them to the cash register. Or, put another way, make sure it'll be a healthy relationship before you ask someone to marry you.

According to a study by the Society of HR Management, "it costs more than a quarter of a million dollars to find and hire a new employee. If that person turns out to be wrong for the role, add to that amount the toll that the bad hire takes on a manager's patience and on colleagues' morale, plus a myriad of other costs if the person needs to be replaced."[4] You can't afford to get it wrong.

Take the time to bring the right people onto the team, create a healthy workplace built on compassion and understanding, influence and inspire, and you will have a team that performs at a higher level with deeper engagement across the board. That's what good leadership looks like.

---

4   Lisa Frye, "The Cost of a Bad Hire Can Be Astronomical," Society for Human Resource Management (May 9, 2017), https://www.shrm.org/resourcesandtools/hr-topics/employee-relations/pages/cost-of-bad-hires.aspx.

BRINGING IT ALL TOGETHER

Leadership is hard. There's no getting around it. As the author Jim Rohn put it, "The challenge of leadership is to be strong, but not rude; be kind, but not weak; be bold, but not bully; be thoughtful, but not lazy; be humble, but not timid; be proud, but not arrogant."

No one steps into a leadership position and says, "Oh, wow, this is so much easier than I thought it would be." And managing sales reps is especially challenging. All of the amazing skills you developed in sales, all of the tactics and techniques that helped you close deals and win over clients, no longer apply.

Almost none of the things that made you a superstar sales rep will make you a good leader, and if you're not prepared, it can be a brutal transition. Sadly, most companies don't do a good job of helping to make that transition. You just get plucked out of sales and put in management, with a pat on the back and a hearty "Good luck. You can do it." They assume you'll do awesome as a sales manager because you're already such an awesome sales rep.

But you find yourself in such a different world that you're soon floundering, just trying to keep your head above water. You were a go-getter, a single-minded, goal-oriented deal-closer. The world was your oyster. You lived for your commissions and your own achievements. Now, you have to be a team-oriented servant who is trying to juggle everyone's needs, goals, and feelings.

I know from experience that this difficult transition can make you hard and embittered, but it doesn't have to be that way. You don't have to fail at leadership. If you'll learn a more "human" way to lead, people *will* start to follow you. Inspire and influence. Lead with empathy. Create your own support network of mentors and peers who can help carry your burdens. Adapt and evolve. You can do it.

Leadership is a choice. As a sales rep, it was all about you— your numbers, your commissions, your awards—but now, you have to *choose* to become a helper. Become someone who wants to make other people shine. Choose to lift others up.

That's hard. Then again, if it was easy, everyone would be in leadership. Hey, sales was hard, too, but you learned the ropes there. Leadership is harder, but you can do it. In this book, I've shared with you how I went from struggling as a leader to making a real impact. I embraced an empathetic, human approach to leadership, and my team rallied around me as a result.

Remember the strategies I shared with you:

- Care about the emotional well-being of your people, even if that means you sometimes have to act like an unlicensed therapist.

- Bring your best self to work. Don't dump your baggage on your employees. That's what your mentors and peers are for.
- If you're getting scary messages from up above, filter some of that fear before passing it along to your team.
- Work on increasing your emotional intelligence, and let your leadership style adapt and evolve with the times.
- You're there to inspire and influence people, not be a puppet master.
- Keep yourself grounded. The ego that made you a good sales rep will not make you a good leader.
- With a bit of patient relationship-building, you can effectively guide and direct even the most high-strung, high-energy sales rep.
- If you place unhealthy expectations on yourself (e.g., working long hours), don't place those same expectations on your team. (And maybe stop placing them on yourself, as well.)
- Who you choose to hire and bring onto the team is just about the most important decision you will make, so for the sake of your team, develop a thoughtful and thorough hiring process.

There's nothing I've done that you can't do, too. Talk with your team about the concepts in this book. Discuss ways to implement them. Let your team members be part of the transition as you work to create a harmonious, functional, effective culture. Start reaching out to potential mentors and peers as you socialize these concepts within your team.

You can do it. People's destinies are in your hand. They're counting on you! Become the leader that they need, a more human and *connected* leader!

ACKNOWLEDGMENTS

My District 10 sales reps, past and present: Shannon, Ryan, Fran, Ashley, Dave, and Matt. You have kept me on my toes and continue to force me to be sharp every day. We win as a team. I appreciate you beyond words.

My father, James "Fuzz" Griffith: You showed me what empathy looked like before I even knew the word. You were the best dad a little girl could have ever had. Thank you for being my hero, and for instilling confidence in me, helping me to understand the pride of a strong work ethic, and making me feel loved even when you weren't 100 percent. I wish I could share this with you now. Thank you for just being you, Pops.

My Zone 2 leadership partners: Kevin, for keeping me "real." Brittany, for helping me continue to be relevant. Steve, for giving me the opportunity to be on the team in the first place. And all of the rest, for being a true work family. You help to make the job not so much of a job.

Paychex: For changing my life in ways you may never know. You took a chance on me in 2017, and I will be forever grateful. Working remotely well before it became a "thing" in 2020.

This amazing organization saved my career. Special thanks to Marty Mucci and Laurie Zaucha for making the decision that allowed me to celebrate in Florida with my peers. It was a truly emotional once-in-a-lifetime night.

Cousin Russell: For always being there in a pinch and always "showing up" when I need an ear. I will be forever grateful that you are in my life and support me unconditionally. Your spices are on point, too.

My brothers, Scott and Mark: Your relentless torment made me gritty. Although hanging me over the balcony was a bit much. Who knew you could get an awesome sister from a Kmart blue light special?

Amanda Cisneros: Sister wife until the end. You inspire me. Thank you for giving me a surrogate father in Pat Jackson and allowing me to be "Aunt Jami" to Mason.

Monica Alsobrook: Fastest running shoes in the West. Thank you, neighbor, for literally saving my life. Your middle name should be 911.

Eric Hendrikx: Thank you for transforming my chaotic thoughts into a coherent speech. Lord knows what I would have said without your guidance.

The Friday afternoon 4:00 Pub Crew: You pushed me to dream a bigger life before I had a clue that there was a life beyond our town's borders. Bruce, Mike, Wes, Roger, Scott, and Jake, thank you for making a young gal feel like she had a future.

Marion Hawkins: You modeled the way for me in more ways than I can tell you.

Michael Majors: You challenged me as a mentor and, moreover, showed me that leadership was much more than just being the boss. You showed me that people matter most.

Barnes: Your quiet presence is appreciated more than you know, buddy. Brother from another mother.

My husband, Carlos: You made us a house and allowed me to focus on my career, and I love you for that. In addition, thank you for the DNA required to create our lovely daughter. She is the best of both of us.

Emily Lord: You are an absolute dream to partner with, lady. Who says sales and service cannot work together in harmony? Thank you for being you, friend.

Jeffrey Miller and the entire Scribe Team: Jeffrey, this book would not have been possible without you. And to everyone at Scribe, I thank you for the guidance and encouragement.

Joey and Michelle Flaherty: Not only did you bring fun into my life while I went through all of the tough stuff, you are special friends that I will always cherish. Thank you for always being there for me.

Terann Johnson: I am so proud to be able to call you my friend now for nearly forty years. We have seen it all together and done it all together. Here is to another four decades of friendship!

Amie Leadingham: I am so inspired by you and your journey. Thank you for being a light in my world and the world.

Dr. Mnatsaknayan, Dr. Michael Muhonen, and Dr. Vadera: Thank you for restoring my brain over and over so I can continue to live my life to the fullest. I promise not to waste the second and third chances you have given me to be alive for my daughter.

Bernie Varela: The best mother-in-law I could have imagined. The kind that turned into a BFF. Love you, Bernadette!

ABOUT THE AUTHOR

JAMI VARELA grew up in Southern California in her early years, until age eleven, then moved to a rural area in the Central Valley in California. After briefly attending college, she dropped out due to unforeseen family financial issues and worked full-time as a waitress in every restaurant she could find. Those years taught her a lot about people and gritty work.

When her mother passed away while Jami was in her twenties and her father moved back to Southern California, she faced her first taste of loss and major adversity. Several years later, in 1999, she decided to leave small-town life and see if she could make it in the "big city." She moved to San Diego, where she secured her first real sales job at the age of thirty. The existence of such jobs surprised her, and she immediately fell in love with the possibilities. Rising from a sales rep to a leader in three years, she found her true calling.

Initially working for a family-owned business, in 2006 she got the opportunity to work at Paychex, which was considered the big league. Despite feeling overwhelmed at first, with support from their world-class training program and a rock-solid mentor, she found her stride. In her first year in sales there, she was named Rookie of the geographical zone she worked in and attained the "Circle of Excellence Award," along with a trip to Maui.

Within the next six months, she was promoted from sales to sales leadership, taking over her sales team. This transition was challenging, but another incredible mentor stepped in to help her launch a successful leadership career. This mentor later became one of the company VPs.

In her fourteen years in this role, Jami qualified for the Sales Conference trip eleven times and ranked in the top five sales leaders four of those eleven years. In 2018, she achieved the number one spot in fiscal following the first of two craniotomies. The first surgery involved the removal of a golf ball–sized brain tumor. The second surgery was a procedure to remove brain tissue that was the site of electrical activity causing continued seizures, even though the full tumor had already been removed. The second procedure worked for a while, but the seizures returned. To this day, she still has active epilepsy.

She showed remarkable resilience through all of this, and following the second brain surgery in 2021, she attained the number two spot in the rankings. These accomplishments during times of extreme adversity were due in large part to the support of her family and friends, both personally and professionally. She focused on what was "possible" and not the negative, making it her mantra to survive and thrive.

This mindset not only spurred her on in the darkest times but also put minor inconveniences into perspective. Motivated to share the ethos she developed, she realized how it opened her to view the world differently and honestly saved her life. She tries to look at every event as a "possibility" and not a roadblock. Viewing people differently too, she acknowledges the many who showed up for her, stood by her, and supported her. She firmly believes that her success would not have been possible without these human connections.